Praise for the HowToDoItFrugally Series of Book for Writers

THE FRUGAL BOOK PROMOTER, SECOND EDITION

"The chapter on perks offered by Amazon is a perfect example of the kind of practical advice offered—the kind that took me months to discover." ~ Rolf Gompertz, author, veteran publicist for NBC, and UCLA instructor

"Newsflash: Whether you self-publish or have a traditional publisher, authors must realize they in fact will be doing the promotion for their book. . . . This book will light the path so that authors can learn how to get that cherished free publicity." ~ Scott Lorenz, Westwind Communications

THE FRUGAL BOOK PROMOTER, FIRST EDITION

"While brainstorming marketing ideas with one of my authors, she informed me she had just purchased the first edition of *The Frugal Book Promoter How to Do What Your Publisher Won't.*

[Because I am a publisher] my immediate reaction was an internal "Oh, no." Then I clicked to Amazon to order it and read up on what it was I wasn't going to be doing! When the neon-yellow book arrived, I devoured it. I was hooked from the first line in Carolyn's acknowledgement: 'Oh, to remember all those who have been instrumental in the birth of a book!' By the time I was done there was as much neon-highlighter yellow inside as it was outside, and, as a fan of Post-its, I made the book look like a yellow-feathered peacock! Carolyn Howard-Johnson has been there, done that in marketing her own books and she packed all her hard-earned wisdom into this Frugal Book series."

~ Nancy Cleary, publisher. Photo of the first edition prickling with Post-it notes also by Nancy Cleary.

THE FRUGAL EDITOR, SECOND EDITION

"Carolyn Howard-Johnson has done it again! Whether you're writing your first book or tenth, *The Frugal Editor* is a must-read." ~ Tim Bete, author and director, Erma Bombeck Writers' Workshop

"*The Frugal Editor* has become an appendage to me." ~ Donna M. McDine, award-winning children's author

HOW TO GET GREAT BOOK REVIEWS FRUGALLY AND ETHICALLY

"This book is a winner! I got a ton of new review opportunities for my authors." ~ L. Diane Wolfe, publisher of Dancing Lemur Press, LLC

GREAT LITTLE LAST-MINUTE EDITING TIPS FOR WRITERS

"I learned a great deal from *Great Little Last-Minute Editing Tips for Writers* and will be referring to it often; I highly recommend it." ~ Karen Cioffi, author, freelance writer

GREAT FIRST-IMPRESSION BOOK PROPOSALS

"'This is a really smart proposal,' was one comment from an agent who went on to sell my nonfiction book to a publisher. The 'smartest' thing about it? I used Carolyn's guide to write it!" ~ Treacy Colbert, medical writer and author of *End Your Menopause Misery*

How to
Get Great Book Reviews
Frugally and Ethically

The ins and outs of using free reviews to build and sustain a writing career

By Carolyn Howard-Johnson

Cover design by Chaz DeSimone

How to Get Great Book Reviews Frugally and Ethically is the third in the multi award-winning HowToDoItFrugally Series of books for writers.

HowToDoItFrugally.com
Los Angeles, California

How to
Get Great Book Reviews
Frugally and Ethically

How to get and use book reviews as part of a viable and ongoing campaign for self-published and traditionally published books

ISBN-13: 978-1536948370
ISBN-10: 1536948373
BISAC: LAN00400, BUS058010

When purchased in quantity, this book is available at a discount to use as premiums, sales promotions, in corporate training programs, by schools, writers conferences, or social organizations, or for other educational purposes. References available on request. For information, please contact HowToDoItFrugally Publishing at HoJoNews@aol.com.

Careers that are not fed die as readily
as any living organism given no sustenance.

Acknowledgements

"Joy keeps writers writing. Gratitude keeps them helping one another." ~CHJ

Once—way back in the early 2000s—when I studied writing at an amazing week-long seminar in St. Petersburg, Russia, with Summer Literary Semesters (sumlitsem.org), a famous and accomplished faculty member scoffed at writers who include a list of those to whom they owe some of their success. He thought the process a ridiculous name-dropping tradition. I thought his lack of gratitude unbecoming, but at the time I didn't know enough about the publishing industry to understand how wrong he was. Publishing—from the printing of a book to its promotion—is a collaborative effort even as we sit in front of our computers on most days considering how solitary the process is.

Those of us who believe we owe our writing careers exclusively to our own talents and motivation must have forgotten our teachers and editors. Forgotten those who help with the publishing process like formatters, book designers, marketers, and other writers like reviewers, bloggers, and members of writers' organizations and critique groups (who tend to be a generous bunch of people who don't constantly remind us how much we owe them). Therefore my thank-you list is long, but probably not long enough.

So, special thanks to writers everywhere—and because of the Web—I do mean *everywhere*. They have come to my aid when asked, but have also offered help when they noticed I needed it. Thanks to my talented cover designer Chaz DeSimone (DeSimoneDesigns.com); my publicists Debra Gold, Rolf Competz, and Marlan Warren; my photographer Uriah Carr, and to all those who cheerfully gave me permission to share their review successes and disasters.

We have all had disasters if we've been around very long. My book of poetry, *Imperfect Echoes* (bit.ly/ImperfectEchoes) was released just after my husband broke his back trouncing around on our roof to save $140 on solar repairs. I became a fulltime caretaker and part time writer and had no time to market my book. I did occasionally send out a query for a review and one was so special that it made up for the sad reality that few will read the book because few will have heard about it. So, thank you to Jim Cox, Editor-in-Chief of Midwest Book Review for that memorable gift.

Once Nancy Cleary sent me a surprise gift more valuable than a dozen roses or a rainbow. It was an adorable banner that included my book covers and award medallions that came in handy because I hadn't yet learned *anything* about photo editing.

I can't forget many who offered their photography and art for the covers of my poetry books. They are Ann Howley, May Lattanzio, Vicki Thomas, Jacquie Schmall, and Richard Conway Jackson who donated art for *Imperfect Echoes* (bit.ly/ImperfectEchoes) and did it from the confines of the California prison system where he is serving twenty-five years to life for receiving stolen property.

Thank you, too, to Joyce Faulkner, Kristie Leigh Maguire, T.C. McMullen, and members of the writing and marketing organizations I belong to who have been generous with their time from the get-go. Oh! And to teachers and mentors like Suzanne Lummis and Eve LaSalle Caram. Writing is a never-ending learning experience.

Special thanks to that husband who falls from roofs, Lance Johnson, author of the award-winning *What Foreigners Need to Know about America from A to Z* (amzn.to/ForeignersAmericaUS). He is never too busy or too sick to apply his organized and unrelenting passion for detail to editing my work and he has had lots of recuperation time to do it.

As for editing, it is crucial to anything a writer puts out where the public can see it. Trudy McMurrin directed several university presses and I was fortunate enough to have her edit my multi award-winning book, *The Frugal Editor* (bit.ly/FrugalEditor) and lend a hand to its original publisher, Red Engine Press. She taught us much about editing as well as the traditional publishers' approach to the niceties of putting a book together—essential things like formatting, pagination, and how much backmatter can do for a writer. She is no longer with us, but I shall be forever grateful to her for her part in the multi award-winning HowToDoItFrugally Series and my writing career.

My apologies to the many others who may have contributed to my success but are not noted.

And special thanks to Bookbaby.com for sharing the e-book version of this book freely with their authors as part of its launch.

Contents

Before We Get Started

> "The old idea that this is the best of times and the worst of times is too simple for publishing. This is the first time since the early days of printing that authors have as much control over their own success as they are ever likely to have." ~ CHJ

Reviews have traditionally been the critiques your book receives from professionals in the publishing industry. In this age of indie films, indie music, and indie publishing we have indie reviewers, too. That is, readers get to critique your work publicly, primarily on online bookstores and blogs.

Reviews can be magic (and they can be downers). They can bring you as much joy (and as much pain) as the actual writing process. They can be the instruments of your book's success. They can inform, change, and mold your future writing technique. Poor reviews (or the lack of reviews) are sometimes blamed for a failed writing career.

If that seems like an overstatement consider this. Marketing is a huge part of a book's success, and getting reviews is a huge part of marketing a book or any other business. If you don't believe it, ask a plumber who has had poor reviews on Yelp!.

Many authors grew up dreaming of one day having a book reviewed in the book section of their local newspaper. It may surprise them that traditional book reviews that once determined the trajectory of a book's success aren't as important as they once were because there are now so many other ways to reach readers beyond traditional bookish journals. We talk about some of those alternatives in this book.

That's not to suggest authors should give up on getting reviews. Authoritative and credible reviews can be influential and one of the most useful tools in your marketing kit.

Most writers think of reviews as a way to inform prospective readers, but when a reviewer cares enough to critique a writer's work—anything from dialogue to structure—it is a precious gift. (Later in this book, we'll talk about ways to assure that they work for you and not against you.) When writers get in a huff and ignore these critiques, they do so at their own peril.

Would you get in a huff? Sure. Go ahead. Have a little tizzy. Get it off your chest (privately). But disregard or discount the critical parts of your reviews? Please don't do that until you have given those critiques careful consideration, maybe even run them by an accomplished writer or editor to see if they think the criticism can be used for the betterment of your next work or if they warrant a rewrite of the book you (perhaps too hurriedly) published on your own.

If you decide the reviewer's input is frivolous or uninformed after you have done due diligence then—and only then—should you discard (and forget) this unpleasant experience. More often reviews will be a source of pride and extremely useful. (This book shows you exactly how to put them to use.)

The review process is both a collaborative and networking effort. When we realize that reviewing—both the getting and giving of reviews—is a way to connect with others in the publishing industry, we become aware that we can learn from those who review our books. If we're smart, we learn from them, keep in touch with them, and call upon them in need.

You may also be surprised that I include a section on *writing* reviews in this book when its title focuses on *getting* them. That discussion includes suggestions for developing your reviewing skills and there are suggestions in Appendix One that will hone your review-writing skills.

So, just why should we care? Well, getting reviews *is* part of marketing a book and that includes the networking aspect of the process. But *writing* reviews can do that for us, too. It's true. *Writing* reviews increases our review-*getting* success incrementally. Many writers may write reviews to help finance their love of writing in the early part of their careers. Sometimes they love doing it and learn so much from doing it that they never give it up. Occasionally it is the writing of reviews that gives them the prestige they seek in the publishing industry.

But here's the best reason for writing reviews of *others'* books: It increases the chances for having our own books read more widely. Yes, that networking thing again, but also the magic of Internet links and Amazon. Keep reading.

We all know that publishing has made cosmic changes in the last decades. In the second edition of my multi award-winning *The Frugal Book Promoter* (bit.ly/FrugalBookPromo), I devote a section on how to get reviews and itemize some new methods that didn't exist in the old traditional-publishing world. It wasn't the good-old-days. Not when a few big publishers had complete control over the publishing of a book and a few big review journals had complete sway over whether a book would sell to bookstores or get shelf space in libraries and therefore be accessible to readers.

I don't have to enumerate how different things are now—in terms of both publishing in general and of getting reviews—because you are in the throes of experiencing them. Thanks to self-publishing. Thanks to online bookstores and their reader reviews. Thanks to both grassroots bloggers and the big, powerful ones with many thousands of subscribers.

Of course, it's always been true that authors who contributed to their own success had a better chance of seeing their writing stars rise and retain their sparkle for a long, long time. Think Charles Dickens. Or don't. Think Mark Twain instead.

Laura Skandera Trombley, president of Pitzer College in Claremont, California, and a noted Mark Twain scholar, says the image we have of this American icon is the one we have "because that's the image [Twain himself] wanted people to have," and that Twain was a man "so gifted at marketing himself that nearly a century after his death, his name still evokes his white-haired likeness."

You can do the same thing given the motivation and the knowledge necessary to sway the media. Reviewers are part of the media. By understanding marketing and PR and knowing the basic skills for getting reviews, we have in our hands the Mark Twain magic—only in many ways the new model offered by the world of computers is enormously more powerful and costs less in both time and money. Today we authors have even more power and control over creating, publishing, and promoting our own books from the moment they're conceived to however long their theme or topic is pertinent. Twain would have been envious.

This book is structured so authors can select chapters that address aspects of their review-getting plan, aspects most needed at any given time. It's meant to function as a perpetual reference for authors who want their books to soar and do not want their careers to languish. It shows authors how the review process can be one of the easiest and most successful tools for making that happen.

If I refer to something covered in depth elsewhere, I give you a prompt for finding it. I also include an Index. I hope it makes it easy for you to find tips for different kinds of review-getting situations as you need them. As an example: When you scan this Index, you may notice the words "media kits" (less accurately known as press kits) and wonder what media kits have to do with reviews. I urge you to use the page indicators to find every entry on that topic in this book. That way you can be sure you are applying the magic of reviews to your media kit in as many ways as possible. Without that cue, you may pass over the references to media kits as you read.

How to Get Great Book Reviews Frugally and Ethically: The ins and outs of using free reviews to build and sustain a writing career is not a textbook. It contains opinions— some as black and white as the page you find them on. It is me talking to you, sharing with you. I had no desire to write a tome that would make people hearken back to their boring high school texts.

I may not cover every possible idea for getting reviews. In fact I avoid anything I have not tried as a professional publicist in promoting my own books, in writing reviews for others' books, and in managing my own *New Book Review* (thenewbookreview.blogspot.com). I started that review blog because I could no longer accommodate all the requests I get from readers of my HowToDoItFrugally series of books for readers. My journalism training comes into play, too. Just as judges are expected to recuse themselves from cases where they may have a vested interest because they can't be considered impartial, so it is for me with writers I know. You will, however, find lots of new (or rarely used) ways to get and use reviews that have not been scorched, stirred, and then warmed over.

Some of my business experience as founder and operator of my own retailing chain comes into play, too. So much of what you learn here will help writers who are also professionals, manufacturers, and business people of any kind. We live in the World Wide Web these days, meaning we are all subject to endorsements and reviews on a wider scale than ever before. I often say, "marketing is marketing is marketing," which is my way of telling you that this book—all my how-to books—are for you, too. Writers can learn tons from other industries—and vice versa.

You must find review-getting paths that fit *your* interests, skills, pocketbook, and your book's title. I expect you to pick and choose from the many suggestions I give you for using reviews. I want my experience to save you time and heartache. I also don't want you to spend money on a review that—if not downright fake—lacks credibility among the gatekeepers that many reviews are meant to persuade.

Fake reviews? Now that I have your attention, keep reading!

Section I
Knowing the Ropes

"Experience is a very good teacher, but contrary to belief, perhaps not the best. Learning what we need before we fail has some obvious benefits." ~ CHJ

You hold this book in your hands because you, my dear reader, know that no matter when we start a new endeavor—be it a new profession or new hobby—we save ourselves lots of time and heartache when we learn as much as possible before we dig in on our own. Of course, we prefer to know the pluses of our new undertaking, but knowing the worst parts beforehand can help us avoid them and help us have more fun with our new venture.

Sometimes having been exposed to something in the past holds more danger than if it's brand new. A little knowledge can lead us to believe we have a handle on it. Reviews—like the one your third grade teacher had you write to prove you read the book she assigned—are like that. Familiarity can give you confidence that leads you astray. When authors see reviews from another perspective they shapeshift. They become part of marketing. And marketing is essential to the success of your new enterprise, your baby, your book.

Chapter One

Book Reviews Aren't What You Think

"The Internet has made this millennium the Wild West of marketing and publishing, and reviews may be the tool that has drifted the farthest from the gentlemanly marketing tool they once were." ~ CHJ

My assertion above is not meant to discourage you from your grand infatuation with getting reviews—reviews like the ones you read a long time ago before you took the trolley, bus, or car to bookstores to buy the must-read of the week. That the review process is different—very different—from what it once was can be either good news or bad news depending on your point of view.

Explaining what reviews *aren't* is the easiest way to dispel mistaken notions authors have about reviews. Still, it helps to know how easy the process is. One of the most intricate review-getting scenarios goes like this:

You ask (query) someone or a media outlet for a review. That someone or media outlet says they are interested and requests a copy of your book. You send your book to that person or media outlet. Your book then gets vetted by your contact or an editor. Your book passes the test. Your book gets offered to that organization's cadre of reviewers (who may or may not accept the review), or it gets assigned to one of that organization's staff or their stable of freelance reviewers. One of those reviewers accepts your book for review. The media outlet sends your book to that reviewer. That reviewer reads your book and writes the review. Your review is published. You may or may not be notified when and where that review may be seen and you may or may not be sent a copy of that review.

This process may sound a little scary to you. You will be glad to know that whether you are traditionally published or self-published, you have a great deal more control over getting reviews for your book than authors ever had before. Here are some major changes:

- Reviewers don't all depend on big media for income anymore.
- Reviewers aren't all professionals anymore. Meaning that they may not be well versed in literature or publishing as a business. In fact, the ones that you will deal with most often—especially if this is your first book—are what have come to be called reader reviewers or amateur reviewers.

- I mentioned before that, contrary to the old model, reviews are no longer essential to getting your book read by anyone other than your mother.

We can thank the Internet for this control authors now have. It offers all kinds of opportunities to get your synopsis and reviews out to bigger numbers than were ever possible when reviews appeared only in prestigious journals like *Library Journal*, *Publishers Weekly*, and *Kirkus* or the book sections of major newspapers like *The Washington Post, Los Angeles Times,* and *The New York Times.*

Media like this—the old media—certainly attract the right eyeballs like librarians (who are big influencers), publishers, bookstore buyers, and, yes, avid readers. But the number of people they reach and the speed with which they reach them are miniscule compared to what a person who knows how to utilize opportunities on the Web can achieve. That person—or persons—can be you or your publicist or the marketing person your publisher assigns to you. Or it can be a combination of all of you.

The Web offers those opportunities up to you like a Thanksgiving turkey on a sterling silver platter. World Wide Web is not called that for nothing. It includes entities like your Web site, your blog (maybe more than one), others' blogs, online news outlets, columnists for online news like *Politico*, online bookstores, online specialty stores, and online trade or business-to-business sites. Granted, some of those online feature editors and columnists may also do double duty for newspapers like

The Wall Street Journal, but many of them don't. We'll discuss how to reach the ones who might be interested in the topic, genre, setting, or any number of other specifics of your book and (another surprise!), those who might be interested in who *you* are, your expertise, even your hobbies (and by extension, your book).

Expectations are trouble-causers. Because we are so involved with the publishing process we may not see the problems reviewers face. That means we are likely to miss opportunities to make it easier on them—and on us.

This blind spot is another reason—and only one of many—why you must think and work ahead to get your reviews. A reviewer must first be convinced that she wants to read your book and, once convinced, she may have a line of books to read ahead of yours. It is up to you to make it as easy for reviewers as possible and to prompt them a bit (tactfully and not too frequently) if the time it takes extends beyond the time frame the reviewer promised.

Kory M. Shrum, an author who has thirty-three reviews on Amazon and eighteen on Goodreads, reminds authors that for a variety of reasons not everyone who promises a review will write one. Those reasons may include:

- Being too busy.
- Getting sick or having an illness befall someone in their family. Life does go on for reviewers, too.
- Finding that he or she is not a match for your book or that she cannot write an honest and credible review for her readers (notice I didn't say "rave" or

"five-star" review) for any other reason including not being fond of your genre.

- Having over-promised in terms of time or workload.
- Lack of organization or making a mistake. (Your book could be under her bed or lost in the bowels of an obscure folder in her computer.)

Shrum says, "If you're expecting twenty to thirty reviews in the first week [after the book is published], you had better plan to request no fewer than 100 to 150 reviews." You will find more on the actual process for sending queries to reviewers in Chapter Five.

Some publishers may be part of the problem. In spite of a contract or even an advance, your publisher may not be a true publisher. True publishing *includes* the marketing of a book. Think big names like HarperCollins and Knopf. They assign a marketing budget to your book and an actual marketing department complete with actual human-type marketers who are trained in the specialized field of not just marketing, but marketing *books*. Except for those who write only for pleasure, there is no reason to publish a book that doesn't get read.

Some publishers—even traditional publishers—may not respect tradition, be uncooperative, or goof. One of my writing critique partners was published with a fine press. When she learned they had not sent advance review copies of her literary novel to the most prestigious review journals before their strict sixteen-week deadline, she was naturally upset. They explained it was a snafu that could not be fixed. That was no comfort at all. It *did* help her to know that because thousands of galleys sent to the important review publications lie fallow in slush piles, the chances of having a book reviewed by a major journal—even one published traditionally let alone getting a glowing review— is remote. Because she had me to nag her, she moved on to alternative marketing and review-getting strategies found in Chapter Six of this book. Using those methods, she was still able to schedule several major bookstore appearances that tend to favor established names and rely on big-journal reviews in their decision-making process. Nevertheless, it's not the kind of loss any author wants to face.

These days most small publishers have no marketing department—or marketing plan. In fact, many admit that when it comes to marketing, you are on your own. No offense, publishers. I know many of you do a terrific job considering the profit margin in publishing these days. Let's face it, you can use help, and you don't need to deal with disappointed (irate?) authors. And, authors! We are ultimately responsible for our own careers. Sometimes when we wait to take responsibility, it is too late in the publishing game.

Some publishers charge the author an additional or separate fee for marketing. Many who offer marketing packages do not offer a review-getting package. If they do, the review their authors get is often a paid-for review, which is definitely *not* the route you want to go. More on that later in this chapter.

It gets worse. Many publishers do not even have lists of people to contact who might help your marketing with endorsements or reviews. As print journals and newspaper book sections shrink or disappear, some larger publishers rely on bloggers for their review process more and more. They're finding that grassroots publicity—reviews or otherwise—can produce a very green crop. And bloggers? Well, that's a resource pool you can easily plumb yourself, and make friends doing it.

My first publisher supplied review copies only upon written request from individual reviewers. They did not honor requests generated by their authors' initiatives. This meant that I could not count on them to supply books to reviewers I had successfully queried for a review. Unless the reviewer accepted e-copies (and many reviewers don't!), I had to order copies directly from the publisher and then reship them to my reviewers. This method is slow, cumbersome, unnecessarily expensive, unprofessional, and discourages authors from trying to get reviews on their own.

Publishers should *offer* review copies to a list of reviewers—even unestablished grassroots bloggers—who have been responsive to their authors in the past. And they certainly should not charge an author for review copies. Publishers have a profit margin and publicity obtained by their authors (including reviews) affects their bottom line, too. They should send their author a thank you (or a red rose!) along with encouragement to keep up the good work.

Publishers should also market their books. That means that even if they are too small or underfunded to have a marketing department, they should have a list of reviewers to query for reviews, a list of influential people to provide blurbs for your cover, access to book cover designers (not just great graphic designers) who know what sells books, and a whole lot more. Ask potential publishers about their marketing process before you sign, but—even if you feel assured after having that conversation—it's best to assume you may be on your own.

So, the marketing part of your book that includes finding the right reviewers to read and comment on your book will—in most cases—be up to you *and* well within your skill set after reading this book. Even when you have the luxury of a marketing department behind you, those authors who know how to get reviews on their own can keep a book alive for an infinite amount of time after their publishers relegate their books to a backlist or their contract expires.

> **Note:** If it is too late to apply this information to the process you use in choosing a publisher, tactfully take hold and guide the publisher you have through the review process. There are lots of ways to do that in this book. I love Nike's advice to "Just do it!" only I add "yourself" to the motto. You may employ your publisher to publish your book or for marketing services. If your book is not truly self-published, it makes money for the publisher when it sells. You don't have to ask for permission (though it never hurts to listen to their reasoning before you make a decision).

Books needn't die. That "infinite" thing I mentioned in the last paragraph means that as long as you are willing to work at marketing it, you can find readers even if it doesn't reach "classic" status. In the old days books were given ninety days to make the grade before bookstores returned them to be unceremoniously relegated to the bargain tables or burned. That may still happen, but as long as you have the copyright you can keep it alive. Or you can revive it when it when sales disappear. One of the best tools for achieving this longevity is getting and promoting reviews . . . and then getting and promoting more reviews.

Reviews can't be bought. And they shouldn't be. At least *credible* reviews can't be bought!

Publisher Rudy Shur (Square One Publishers) says "We have found that [paid-for] reviews practically scream 'self-published book' to those in the trade. We feel they result in a perception of a book as being something less than [professional.]" Those who have read my other books or subscribe to my SharingwithWriters newsletter (bit.ly/SWWNewsletter) know that in terms of journalism ethics, paid-for reviews are questionable, even unethical. How can someone you paid write a fair and honest review? Everyone knows it's practically impossible. Even if an author is lucky enough to get a *fair* rave review, it will still be suspect. Authors who buy reviews spend their valuable promotion budget on something that doesn't impress anybody, even most readers.

Richard Carmen, publisher at Auricle Ink in Sedona, AZ, gives us another reason that paid-for reviews aren't worth the money. He says, " . . . unless you have a near-blockbuster, the reviews [from major review journals] . . . lack the positive punch that sells a book . . . ." I find the same thing with the paid-for reviews at Kirkham and most of the other reviews in it, too.

REVIEW-TRIPPERS

There is a whole battery of things that trip up authors who are publishing the first time (or maybe the twelfth!)—no matter what kind of press their book is being published on. Many of these review-trippers confound small publishers and I have seen a few of them trip up large publishers, too. They are:

1. The unreasonable lead-time for receiving book review queries imposed by big, traditional, and prestigious review media. (Learn more about why they do so later in this chapter.)

> **Missed deadlines** aren't the end of the world. When deadlines are missed, authors often feel hopeless and when deadlines aren't missed authors often become discouraged if their book is not accepted. This is the number-one tripper I see among new authors and I'll explain how to abide by the rules—and get around them—later in Chapter Six, "Magic Bullets for Getting Reviews."

2. Most of those same journals practice what many consider book bigotry. That is, they judge books submitted to them for reviews based on who published them rather than the quality of their content.

Note: Exceptions sometimes happen. Know that occasionally indie publishers (that includes partner-, small- and self-publishers) do get attention from these entities but only when they have produced quality books that have literary or commercial merit and their submission process follows industry standards.

3. The misconception that publicity (including reviews) automatically results in book sales.

Note: Media exposure is not a guaranteed miracle worker. It helps to know right up front that any kind of marketing—advertising, publicity, speaking or whatever—rarely works on its own. Marketing is about persistence. Marketing builds on itself. Your efforts bear fruit when you know you're in this for the long haul, and you'll find more joy in the process when you don't have unrealistic expectations for any given promotion.

4. The misguided idea that authors must have a book in print before they can ask for reviews.

Note: The digital age means there are alternatives never once dreamed of—including publishing itself—and actually makes some processes easier than they ever were before. Much of this book elaborates on the "teaspoonsful of sugar" that make this kind of medicine go down—some in this chapter. Know, however, that with knowledge (and experience), there is almost no barrier for getting reviews or getting around other conundrums that can't be overcome. Ethically.

5. Reviews and book sales do not necessarily correlate as well as one would expect. In review tripper number three above you learn that they work cumulatively and in conjunction with other marketing. I have a traditionally published friend whose book was reviewed by *Newsweek* (back in the days when it was published worldwide in print and its reach was arguably unparalleled), and her book still did not earn royalties over her advance.

AUTHORS OFTEN AREN'T FAMILIAR WITH THE ARC CONCEPT

I talk about preplanning often in this book because human beings (including authors) play the waiting game. Procrastination is about review-tripper number four. It seems logical that you need a book available online or in print for reviewers to *read*. But you needn't wait to have proof copies or ARCs (advance reader—or reviewer—copies) before you can ask for reviews. Authors who listen to rumors may miss the opportunity to pitch a review to big review journals or to get exciting blurbs for the backs of their books.

The kind of copy you are expected to provide to a reviewer depends on the kind of reviews you are trying to get, of course, but even the most sought after review journals may accept manuscripts in lieu of finished books or digitally printed ARCs. Those journals that accept these manuscripts (often called galleys—a term left over from the days when all printing was done on offset presses) often require that you send a finished book once one is available. They need proof that the book is available to their readers before they run their presses. It's extra work for you, but worth it to know that your manuscript may be sufficient to get the review ball rolling. It also helps your marketing campaign to know that some magazines and journals work on each issue six months in advance. When I was working at *Good Housekeeping*, we started our decision-making even earlier.

We'll talk more about getting these early reviews and others later in this book, but know it is almost never too early—or too late in this new age of publishing—to start working on the review process for your book.

Next up! We'll discuss why you should be eager to get reviews on your own regardless of the efforts made by your publisher.

Chapter Two

Why You Need To Get Reviews

"Reviews, like the right kind of love, are forever—thanks to the Web." ~ CHJ

The publishing world is a'changin'. You might get by without a single review and still sell a ton of books by concentrating all your promotion efforts online (though that could include reviews, too).

I'm thinking of many of the methods I include in my multi award-winning *The Frugal Book Promoter* (bit.ly/FrugalBookPromo). Things like providing so much valuable content on your Web site that it becomes a go-to portal for anyone interested in the topic you write about (and, yes, this works for fiction writers, too). Things like using forums and other places where people interested in your topic hang out—places like Yahoo groups or AuthorU's forum at LinkedIn. Like using benefits offered by online bookstore giants—Amazon.com in particular—where you can do it worldwide.

But why would you want to get by without reviews?

Reviews can get repurposed so many ways. Here are ways they can make your book—and entire career—soar!

REVIEWS ARE POWERFUL CAREER BUILDERS

If you use reviews to their full potential, they are more than a means to getting readers. Later in Section V of this book, you'll learn how even writing reviews for others' books can benefit yours and benefit your entire writing career. Here are a few ways you can help them work for you from the get-go.

Forget positive vs. negative reviews. What constitutes great reviews is not positive or negative, five-star or . . . ahem . . . just so much garbage. Authors should view what the reviewer has to say—no matter what it is—as an opportunity to become a better writer, to know their genre better, to understand the demographic they write for better, and on and on. There is no limit to the possibilities that might come to light in a single review, and sometimes the most painful reviews are the ones that do us the most good.

To illustrate my point, I'll tell you a little story. (Many of us writers are storytellers at heart, right?) I review products for Amazon as one of their Vine reviewers and was offered a jar of Penetrex as part of that program. It is a product that helps soothe sore muscles and my husband had just fallen from our roof and crushed five vertebrae. He's as frugal as I am and wanted to save $150 repair bill on our solar panels. My grandmother used to quote Robert Burton when she thought she was quoting Benjamin Franklin, but the sentiment is still appropriate. She said, "Penny wise and pound foolish." She said it a lot. She loved my husband.

Both my husband and I loved the product, but I have been on a bit of a vendetta about products that are formulated with Vitamin E but don't specify exactly which of the E tocopherols they use or unabashedly list tocopherol acetate as if it is an all-natural ingredient. Tocopherol acetate is *not* natural. It is often processed using harsh chemicals that are systemic and can be extremely damaging for some people. So, I mentioned that in my review. As much as we liked Penetrex, we would not—could not—use it once we realized that tocopherol acetate was the culprit behind his systemic inflammation.

To the credit of Biomax Health Products, the maker of Penetrex, I received an e-mail from Pamela Weiss, the Vice President of that company. She framed her note as a thank you and mentioned the company's dedication to helping others by saying, "We can't thank you enough for taking the time [and] effort to share your experience with Penetrex. It is a very special formulation which we are all very proud of [and] you should take pride in knowing that your review will go a VERY long way in helping others find relief."

She then mentioned that the company had indeed switched to natural tocopherols! She said, "You'll be happy to know that we listen to the voice of the Penetrex community and are switching from tocopherol acetate to tocopherol (natural Vitamin E). [Our] chemist was finally able to make this happen for us."

She also delicately alluded to the status of the review (not a five-star!) without violating the rule that a review must be "honest and fair." Because it was only the tocopherol situation that caused me to downgrade the rating anyway, I didn't feel her letter was a violation of review ethics.

> **Note:** Ms. Weiss's letter is a model for an ideal thank you in the face of a less-than-rave review. It is also a perfect example of public relations as it was taught in a class I took at the University of Southern California. In the face of adversity, the job of PR is to face the problem *immediately*, to admit wrongdoing deliberately and sincerely (no namby-pamby excuses!), and to make amends (perhaps an assurance that you will use their idea in the future or make changes in your next edition).

Reviews are resources for endorsements. These are sometimes called blurbs, praise, and—rarely—bullets.

When my husband and I go to the Laemmle to see independent films we see people standing in front of attractive movie posters rapturously taking in every word printed on them. Those "words" are usually excerpts from reviews written about the film. Authors can take excerpts from their reviews and use them in much the same way. For us that would mean using them on posters used at book fairs, tradeshows, and book signings.

To excerpt these little marketing treasures from reviews to use in your marketing, extract a sentence, phrase, or inspirational adjective like "rapturous" from the greatest reviews you get, put them in quotes and add a credit, either the name of the review journal, the name of the reviewer, or both. Here's an example of one I used from one of my favorite reviews for my book of poetry, *Imperfect Echoes* (bit.ly/ImperfectEchoes):

> " . . . articulate, gifted, insightful, iconoclastic, and a truly impressive literary talent . . . an inherently fascinating, thoughtful, and thought-provoking read . . . highly recommended . . . ." ~ Jim Cox, Editor-in-Chief of *Midwest Book Review*.

You can see how I use ellipses where I left out connecting words. Depending on how the blurb is used, you may want to be sure the title of your book is in the blurb. If you must add something like a title that wasn't originally used by the reviewer, install that phrase inside brackets like these: [ ].

> **Note:** I sometimes use portions of this excerpt in different ways. The first part alludes to my poetry in general. The second specifically to the book Cox reviewed.

When you reprint an excerpt, keep it to twenty-five words or fewer. Though I used more in the example above, twenty-five is the limit Amazon's guidelines allow to assure that reviewers and authors stay within free-use copyright guidelines when they install blurbs (excerpts) on sales or buy pages. In view of the complexity of copyright law, it is a rule of thumb as good as any I've run across.

> **Tip**: You can add blurbs to your Amazon buy page easily by going to Amazon's Author Connect feature (formerly known as Author Central) where you will find many possibilities for prettying up your book's page and making it a more efficient sales tool.

Because of its brevity and emotional power, this blurb for Jaguar's XE is one of my favorite blurbs excerpted from a review:

> "Suspension from the Gods . . . ." ~ *Road & Track*

You can use portions of reviews (excerpts) as endorsements or blurbs in lots of other places, too, including:

- On the page just inside the front cover of the next edition or updated copy of your book.
- On the first page of your title's e-book right now. Immediate changes are one of the advantages of e-books over print.
- In your query letters that go out to about everyone including radio hosts, newspaper and magazine feature editors, and coordinators for reading groups.
- On a special page of "praise" in your media kit. (See my *The Frugal Book Promoter* (bit.ly/FrugalBookPromo) for step-by-step instructions on building a media kit, and notice how I make media kits do double duty in this book's Chapter Thirteen on staying motivated.)

- In about everything you use for promotion:
  - o Your newsletter, blog posts, Web site, e-mail signature.
  - o In your stationery letterhead (or footer).
  - o In the handouts you use when you speak at conventions or tradeshows or the fliers you hand out at book fairs.

Learn about other ways to use endorsements and blurbs that you extract from reviews (or get independently from celebrities and well-known experts in the field that you write about) in Section IV of this book, "You Have Your Review. Now what?"

Reviews can be networking tools. One of the most valuable ways to build lasting relationships with others in the publishing industry is by getting reviews *and* writing reviews of books you've read and loved, found useful, or of books in your own genre.

The review process (getting or giving) includes networking possibilities like these:

- Contacts with the editors of review journals.
- Contacts with other reviewers who may someday be open to reviewing your books. Because reviewers often (usually!) write books or freelance, they also may have connections with agents and with acquisition editors at publishing houses.
- Contacts with other authors who use social networks, need quotations for their books, sometimes include suggested reading in their

appendices, and on and on. Most authors realize we are all in this together and often help one another with referrals.

Getting *credible* reviews should be one of your review-getting goals and *you* are likely the person who knows (or knows of) those whose endorsements would influence the most people interested in your topic, theme, or genre.

You are also the one most likely to be committed to the effort it takes to get reviews in trusted review journals. I talk about how you pursue these journals—equivalent in the review world to the Holy Grail—in Chapter One and I give you information on how to circumvent their stringent guidelines when you need to in Chapter Six under "Legitimate Hacks."

Reviews are a better choice than advertising. The publishing industry and literary gatekeepers trust them and they're *free* except for your time, the cost of shipping, and the (wholesale) cost of a book. (Those last two expenses can be taken as deductions on your United States income tax forms.)

The most important reason, though, is that reviews are *more effective* (I already said lots more frugal, right?) than advertising. Trust me. Studies bear out what I learned the hard way—from experience.

That's not to say that gatekeepers don't pay attention to certain ads. Bookstores, as an example, notice large (read that expensive!) ads in influential periodicals because they surmise there is a hefty marketing budget behind that particular title. They appreciate support that helps drive traffic to their stores. They also know that authors and publishers—even the big publishers who place those ads— are aware that other kinds of marketing are more frugal. Lots more frugal. And more effective in most other ways. (Big publishers may believe they must support the journals that have yay-or-nay power over publishing reviews.)

Other advantages for getting reviews:

- Reviews are an integral part of your book's marketing campaign—from book tours to blurbs on book covers.
- If the reviews you get take hold and catch the interest of bookstore buyers and librarians, your book sales may snowball.
- The more places your title is seen, the more likely individual readers will buy it. It's part of marketing. It's exposure. It's about frequency. You can work on frequent exposure by using reviews because the best ones never cost more than a book, shipping, and your time.
- You'll need to get what are known variably as blurbs, bullets, or endorsements anyway. Look at it this way: Getting a review from which you can take excerpts, too, takes very little additional time.
- The query letter you wrote to get a publisher or an agent need only be adapted a little to make it work for reviews, too.

AMAZON INCREASES THE NEED FOR REVIEWS

Amazon is a career builder and a powerful sales machine for books all on its own, but its existence increases the need for great reviews incrementally.

Publicity Hound Joan Stewart (publicityhound.com) says, "If you can eventually amass more than 100 legitimate reviews on Amazon.com, [that powerful online bookstore] will consider paying for Google pay-per-click ads and ads on Facebook and other sites to pull people onto your Amazon sales pages." Amazon reviews are mostly reader reviews and they're the easy ones to get. Often all you need do is ask folks you know who have read your book to write one and post it. We'll talk more about other ways Amazon reviews can be managed to benefit your book later in Chapter Eleven, "Managing Your Amazon Reviews."

Reviews grow footprints on Google, Bing, and Goodsearch. You can use free services like Addme.com to get your Web site listed on these and other search engines, but you'll need to use the chapter on doctoring up your Amazon page to do the same for Amazon. And, yes, Amazon is a search engine, too.

Not to get too techy on you, but the mentions you get in reviews optimize your search engine optimization (SEO) stats and help you get general exposure for your book and for you as a writer.

If you don't believe search engine optimization (meaning little tricks to make search engines work in your favor) can help you, this is an example: I hadn't seen or heard from one of the editors who mentored me as a journalist when I first started writing more than a decade ago. Out of the blue, I received an e-mail from her. When I marveled at how glad I was to hear from her, she explained, "You aren't exactly hard to find with a Google search." Obviously, SEO works in ways we can't imagine. Do be careful about giving out personal information like home addresses and personal telephone numbers that might sneakily become a destructive Google entry

The secret to keeping this query-letter writing, review-getting, excerpt-gleaning, networking process rolling at a clip is to keep your marketing bonnet on. Adding a media outlet or name to one of your contact lists when it occurs to you doesn't take much time; if you wait to do it all at once you'll have a project that never gets done, or you'll forget, or you'll . . . you get the idea. This is a process, *not* a project. Your diligence will come in handy for the book you are currently writing, your next, and your next. We talk about the process of growing and organizing your contact list for reviewers in this book, too.

You are ready to tackle getting your first book review or more reviews than you now have (no matter where you are in the publishing process). Reviews are like diamonds; their luster stays and stays. So let's move on to the big bugaboo in the process we all face to one degree or another—book bigotry.

Chapter Three
Getting Past Book Bigotry

"Indie publishing, like indie films, is finally earning a reputation for creativity and serving niche audiences." ~ CHJ

I've personally watched how attitudes toward self- and indie-publishers—like a lot of other controversial topics—have become more accepting over the past couple of decades. Not so very long ago an author who was published by anyone other than university presses and New York's Big Five were derisively called "vanity publishers," and I rarely—thankfully—see that term used anymore. Still, book bigotry or its near cousins (a few of those would be racism, snobbery, prejudice, sexism, and chauvinism) haven't disappeared. Yet.

Brook Warner, board member at Independent Book Publishers of America (IBPA-online.org) and author of *Green Light Your Book* (bit.ly/GreenLightBook) says, "I advise authors with POD (print-on-demand)-printed books never to specify how their books were printed. If you're talking to book buyers, event hosts, booksellers, conference organizers, or librarians, leave that part out."

That she finds it necessary to give that advice is discouraging, but she is addressing reality. Some—including reviewers—find it convenient to let the name of a press vet their choices among hundreds of thousands of books available to them these days. Using the name of a respected press is an easy—though misguided—way to do that.

Notice that Warner is not suggesting you fib about how the book is published. In many cases it may be judicious to simply avoid mentioning the publisher. The trouble is, you probably won't fool anybody. Professionals will notice the absence of this information and guess why you didn't include it, and a big percentage of readers won't care anyway.

Alternatively, you can form a publishing house to publish your own books exclusively, or one that publishes a select few books each year—your own and others' as well. Small publishers like these are often referred to as micro presses. The how-tos for this are in the purview of another entire book, but it won't be a book of mine. I know of only one author who has done it successfully and have heard of only a few others. I believe most indie authors would be better off expending time, talent, and energy on their own books and will be happier for it.

Warner also says that in some instances you should bravely face down book bigotry. By that she means owning up to however your book is published. Defending it without being defensive. I like this advice better.

My coauthor of the Celebration Series of Chapbooks, Magdalena Ball, and I list our books in that series (bit.ly/CarolynsPoetryBooks) in our media kit as "Proudly independently published in the time-honored tradition of poets since before Gutenberg invented the press."

We writers know that words and the way we use them are powerful and we should be willing to use that power within the boundaries required by ethics.

It is your job—no matter who printed your book—to convince reviewers (and, yes, readers and media gatekeepers!) that your book is *the* one they want to spend time with. That your book has value that a particular reader or reviewer can use, wants, or desperately needs. To do that, we need to get by their vetting process and you do that by:

- Publishing or having someone else publish a professional, well edited book. Read more on how to do that in my multi award-winning *The Frugal Editor* (bit.ly/FrugalEditor) and find more books that will help you with that journey in the Appendices of this book.
- Building—and continuing to build—a platform that is respected by others in the publishing industry.

(Read more on that in *The Frugal Book Promoter,* bit.ly/FrugalBookPromo.)

- Approach reviewers with whom you have built a relationship and/or those you have vetted so carefully you are confident that they have an interest in your genre. That requires lots of research, but you won't waste sending a book to someone with no clout or who isn't actually a reviewer (more on that in Chapter Four titled "Free Books, Shifty Reviewers, and Other Scams"). The care you take also limits the chances of your content being misused. For more on that, see Chapter One, "Book Reviews Aren't What You Think," and Chapter Four in this book.

> **Note:** If you are a self-publisher or are publishing with a small or obscure press and are having trouble getting past gatekeepers who assume your book is not worthy because it doesn't carry the name of a big publishing house, don't assume that authors published by big publishing houses don't sometimes feel the same way. The New York Big Five publishers sometimes have trouble finding the right review or enough reviews for a book, too. They've also been known to make mistakes that put their clients' books in jeopardy. I know because I've seen it happen.

You, the author of your book, are the one who is so passionate about it you will not be daunted by the review-garnering task. In the process, you pretend you are a florist and put the best blooms in your book bouquet forward. You discard the wilted ones, or at least place them behind the more exquisite blossoms in your inventory.

Note: I fervently combat book bigotry whenever I get the chance and hope you will join me with that task no matter who published your book. I registered the hashtag #bookbigotry with Twubs.com. If you have something to add to the book bigotry conversation, use it in a few of your tweets so it will appear on my hashtag page (twubs.com/BookBigotry). It will help you get more exposure on the World Wide Web. While we're talking about it, if you ping me with @frugalbookpromo when you tweet book news, I'll like it and retweet it, too!

Chapter Four

Free Books, Shifty Reviewers, and Other Scams

> "'Buyer beware' never felt truer than it does to authors starting out in an industry that is new to them. The trick is discerning perceived dangers from real dangers and the extent of the latter." ~ CHJ

Remember Mary Englebreit? She's the greeting card artist who drew a feisty little girl who stamped her foot and said, "Get over it." This is the chapter that helps you manage your fears (and your frugal book budget). It is here to help you avoid all the aspects of getting reviews you most want to avoid or at least make the ones you can't avoid more palatable. Englebreit would agree you can "get over" just about anything you understand better.

SENDING YOUR BOOK TO STRANGERS

The idea of letting anyone—even professionals—get a glimpse of your precious upcoming book may seem a foreign concept to you.

People you don't know might steal your ideas or plagiarize your work. You may be especially worried about letting them see it before it's published. In fact, you may be having nightmares about it.

This fear isn't limited to the review process. Fear of plagiarism is a topic of discussion among the writers I meet on the Web, in my critique groups, in my classes, or wherever authors get together to further their careers. Some writers are crippled by fears of all kinds but this fear is more damaging than most others.

It's *this* fear that keeps some from sending their manuscripts to publishers and agents, from trusting professional editors and teachers to advise them, and from seeking spotlights that might assure the success of their books.

Of course, you should take precautions, but worrying about plagiarism or giving away an idea instead of focusing on the joy of sharing your talent with others can be destructive to both your creativity and to the business of building your career in the publishing world. I would rather have a million people read one of my poems in a Dear Abby column credited only as "Anonymous" than have it read not at all. Having our voices heard is more important than selling books. Having our voices heard is sharing our souls. I fervently hope more writers will come to share this view.

The kind of plagiarism that authors worry about is quite rare. It's hard to steal an idea. For one thing, there are no truly new ideas in the world. If you don't believe me, read Joseph Campbell's works (which you should do anyway). He divides all of literature from Greek plays onward into a few categories with a few basic elements. It's unlikely your work is so unique that it doesn't fit into one of them.

Further, ideas cannot be copyrighted. A recent court case reaffirmed this notion. If it had not, much of Shakespeare's works would be considered plagiarism and, because science fiction writers often borrow theories from those who win Nobel prizes in physics, that genre could no longer exist as we know it.

Many kinds of borrowings are not plagiarism but the result of the similar way our brains function. You've probably heard the story of monkey colonies on one island who take up the same habits of monkeys on another island with no understandable way for them to have communicated.

You should know that anyone who uses your idea—including a prospective reviewer—would surely write a different book than yours. Bolster your confidence by trying this exercise: Ask three writers to pen a piece using a very specific subject—maybe even something you've considered writing yourself. My critique group used a story about how, as a child, one of our members sneaked into a neighbor's house and ate frosted strawberries out of the

Fridge. We then set a lunch date and read each work aloud. In spite of the similar plot lines, the voices, characters, and details were so different we wondered why we had been concerned about a fellow writer stealing an idea. Usually, a writer won't be interested in writing someone else's stuff, anyway. Most writing, after all, is about *self*-expression.

Often when a case of plagiarism occurs among those who have the public trust, it gets lots of press. However, by the time the perpetrator is found innocent, the case has lost its news value, and we never hear about the accused's exoneration. Thus, authors feel bombarded with reports of plagiarism-that-never-happened.

Plagiarism is most rampant in academia. If you need proof, google "plagiarism." Yep, a few famous cases and lots more stories about kids trying to make the grade at school. We cannot condone such theft, but we authors should not allow the idea of plagiarism to doom the progress of our writing careers. Generally it is only the poor naïve (or dishonest) student or writer who grabbed down someone else's work who suffers—whether or not he is caught.

Another consideration. If someone should swipe a few of your words or an idea, his chances of becoming rich, famous, and envied because of them are no better than yours. If he should, that sets him up for legal action worth pursuing. If he doesn't get rich on your work, you have the satisfaction of knowing he didn't and won't need to bother your talented head about chasing after a pauper. You might even benefit. The publicity surrounding such a case could be the lucky stroke that makes *you* the rich, famous, and envied author.

Simply put, you take precautions. You copyright your work at the Library of Congress site (loc.gov). When you are researching the reviewer you hope will review your book, you check a couple journals or Web sites where she publishes the reviews she writes. Don't worry too much. This process is more about getting a handle on whether your book will actually be reviewed and will be published somewhere—a prestigious journal or online at Amazon, Goodreads, or the reviewer's own blog. If you've done even rudimentary research your chances of being plagiarized or wasting a good book on someone who was only fishing for a freebie will be reduced even more.

PAYING FOR ALL THOSE FREE BOOKS

I know. Brrr. The idea of giving away a book you toiled over and loved may not appeal to you. The idea might tempt you into trying to con reviewers into accepting an e-copy rather than a paperback or ARC.

Don't do it.

In fact, try not to think of it this way. You are getting at least as much for the cost of your book from the reviewer including reading, writing, and posting time.

For one thing e-books are more dangerous in terms of copy-and-paste plagiarizing than a print book. It seems that someone who plagiarizes is inherently lazy and it is a lot easier to copy-and-paste from an e-copy than it is to type a chosen sentence, paragraph, or book from scratch. But the real reason you want to give a reviewer a copy of your book in the format they prefer is that you want her to be happy reading it.

I am a Vine reviewer for Amazon.com and I can tell you from experience that I am not as favorably influenced when a company skimps on sending the instruction booklet that goes with, say, a piece of exercise equipment. Books are products, too. A reviewer will be subtly prejudiced against a book with a crumpled cover or one that shows up with no cover letter, sell sheet, or media kit. (Not to worry. More is coming on how to make a great impression whenever you might need to send a review copy.)

Some reviewers go to pains to remind you not to "deface" your review copy in any way. *Midwest Book Review* is one of those. They ask you not to mark or label it as a review copy. Try to think of it this way: A reviewer is giving you a gift. They put hours into reading your book and more time and consideration into writing the review. Often (not always) their pay is only the book you send them. If they should decide to pass along your book to charity or to a friend, they are doing you a favor. That sharing of your book is a recommendation for your book, and the more people who see your book, read your book, like your book, and tell someone else about your book, the more successful your book will be.

PAY-FOR REVIEW SCAMS ABOUND

Authors are a profitable target for scam artists because the publishing industry is burgeoning. There are just so many naïve authors to rope in. Because so many of them are new at publishing, they often can't discern real help from . . . er, disingenuous offers.

Some who offer that help—help like pay-for reviews—are well-intentioned folks. They may even be hard-working writers trying to make additional income. Some are out-and-out cons. Regardless of their motives, they lure authors who believe their books are doomed to failure without reviews into these little-or-no value schemes.

There may be a few pay-for review services that are worth the money—in particular those that package the review you pay for with other services—but think about it. It is difficult for a reviewer employed by the author or publisher of that book not to be influenced by that relationship. When readers or industry influencers aren't sure they are getting honest reviews, they don't consider them credible. That is why paid-for reviews fly in the face of accepted journalism ethics.

Most of these paid-for-review plans are out-and-out scams even when they are offered by reputable journals. Booksellers, librarians, and some readers know paid-for reviews when they see them (even when they see them in *Kirkus* and *Publishers Weekly*).

Reviews in these trusted journals can easily cost $400 or more. They are often relegated to inferior status in the very same journals that are happy to take your hard-earned money for the privilege of giving you such shabby service. By that, I mean they put them into a section apart from the legitimate "honest and fair" reviews.

Some offer special stars or praise to a select few of their authors who have paid for reviews. So few of those books are so honored that the system smacks of the snake-oil promises of old. Buy first and learn how useless the product is later. In the meantime, the unfortunate author's book is devalued in the eyes of the very gatekeepers the author is trying to impress by spending their advance or out-of-pocket money on a review.

Paid-for reviews are especially lamentable because there is no need to put yourself in a regrettable position like this. Authors can tweet a request for a book review. You offer a copy of your beautiful book in exchange for a review and will probably get more acceptances than you bargained for. These reader reviews may not appear in the big journals, but they can be used in all the ways an in-the-know author uses reviews for and they are likely to be more honest.

Authors often get tricked into buying (and participating in) all kinds of promotional services that are unethical, don't sell many books, and aren't useful as lasting marketing practices. One such scam from a well-known publisher offers to send your book to Oprah—including guaranteed delivery, but—of course—they don't guarantee that she will look at it. I picture your book arriving on her threshold in a box with books of fifty other hopeful (and gullible authors—a box that will immediately get sent to Goodwill or returned). I could mention other such "opportunities," but I don't want to give them any traction. As they say, "Buyer beware." Now you know they are rampant you'll be more likely to know 'em when you see 'em—even if they have nothing to do with reviews.

Review-and-opinion sites, online bookstores, and online popularity contests like the annual one run by Preditors and Editors that seems to encourage ballot box stuffing do a disservice to the publishing industry as a whole. You waste your time corralling votes for an "honor" that has no credibility. I've also seen real benefits offered by Web sites like Amazon.com disappear after authors abused them.

Be alert to anything that feels manipulative. If your book is going nowhere, do something positive for it instead. Take a writing class. Go to a conference on publishing like the one IBPA (Independent Book Publishers of America) offers every year to learn more about the industry you have chosen to be part of. Learn the time-honored publicity techniques in *The Frugal Book Promoter* (bit.ly/FrugalBookPromo). Learn more about how to maximize the effect of the reviews you want—the ones you can get without paying someone to rave about your work. I show you how to do that in the next few chapters of this book. Your career will soar—ethically.

Section II
Starting Early and Building

"It's never too early or too late to begin building the foundation you'll need to maximize your ability to get reviews." — CHJ

As publishers' budgets have gotten slimmer, making a living from selling books has gotten tougher. To help their bottom line, most call on their authors to help them get reviews or turn the marketing process over to them entirely. Getting reviews—if done right—is an important part of marketing, and it is very nearly free except for the time you need to research the media most suited to your book and other aspects of your career.

The best time to prepare for getting great reviews is right now. Yes, even if your book is just a dream that keeps nudging you to take action.

The earlier you start, the better prepared you will be and better prepared you are, the more effective you'll be. Getting great reviews is about relationships, about sharing your passion with others. This section removes that nagging question of where you start your review-getting and marketing process and how to put your passion for writing and publishing to work in a way that makes this "sharing" part a reality.

Chapter Five

Find Reviewers and Make Lists Now

> "Building contact lists may be the only addiction you'll ever want to acquire. They are your forever support system, and they work best for the author who persists well beyond a book's release." ~ CHJ

Contact lists are like friends. You need a whole lot more than one. Sometimes you'll call your lists something else like "newsletter subscriber file," "Christmas card list," "writers' group membership rosters," or "block-party neighbors list." They're all contact lists, and most will have lots of folks on them who will become your readers . . . and reviewers. You'll learn to code each person on those lists for either category or both, and those newly coded lists will become your list-of-lists so to speak in terms of importance for the welfare of your book.

You will not use your list of reviewers only when you're launching a new book. Primarily because of the Web, we can keep our books alive forever—all of them from the first to the one that's about ready to be published. When sales on a book start to lag, your list of reviewers comes in handy once again.

But so do your other lists. Some people think of themselves as reviewers (or you think of them that way). But some readers review, too, or can be encouraged to become reviewers. Some authors review. So do some journalists, freelance writers . . . well, you get the idea. So your general contact lists of your readers, of your fellow authors, even of your personal friends can come in handy when your book needs exposure—and getting reviews is one way to get that exposure. Your lists may also come in handy when you need help with some other aspect of your writing career.

There are three ways to build any list. Buy a list from businesses like American Express, assemble a list from online and library resources, and build your own list as you come in contact with folks—everyone from readers to editors to new media outlets to reviewers. Of course, you can—and should—use whatever lists are most appropriate for any project. But you'll find the list you build yourself will reap the most rewards—by far.

THE LIST YOU BUILD YOURSELF

You automatically have a better handle on a list you build yourself than one you rent, borrow, or buy. You will know something—a little or a lot—about every entry on your do-it-yourself list.

We all know what building relationships is. Relationships are all around you from your family to people you know on Facebook but have never met in person. This list you build yourself starts with today's relationships and builds from there.

In the business world (publishing is a business and, yes, writers are part of that industry), we often call building relationships "networking" . . . and that's what you are doing when you build a contact list of people you know and media you are familiar with. With the advent of the Net the possibilities for relationships are so much greater than they once were and have become even more important to success. Nowhere are they more important than in getting reviews.

So, isn't it nice that building a contact list is one of the first things an author can do to help assure her marketing campaign has a great foundation before her book is published and that those sought-after reviews will be easier to get!

Knowing something about each person helps you send your message only to the specific group who will be interested in it. Though marketing studies vary, studies have shown that results from hand-built contact lists are up to ten times or more effective than buying or borrowing others' lists.

So, this is your *frugal* guide to getting reviews. Why would you buy a list from another author, Web site, or service when you can build a better list in just a minute or so a day.

.

To keep track of all your contacts including reviewers and review media, label (or categorize) entries in your database so you know the names of reviewers but also the journals, book review sections or whatever they work for (or freelance for), and where they are located. If you build your list on your own, a good portion of it will be made of reviewers and media you know well or soon will know well. The better you know a person or a medium, the better you'll understand how to pitch ideas to them.

Gathering entries for your list requires that you nurture a tuning-in process that you put to work when you're watching TV, listening to radio, traveling or . . . just living. Make notes. Google the medium or contact as soon as you can after running across it, and keep building that database one entry at a time. I have been known to tear contact information out of magazines and newspapers, stuff them in my bra, and retrieve them when they flutter to the floor as I get ready for bed at night. I kid you not!

So, you are on the lookout for media when you're out and about. You run across a newspaper, a magazine, or even a throwaway (remember what we said about finding important information where we least expect it?). You put your thinking bonnet on. "Aha!" you say. "This little community weekly may be interested in my story because it's just for women . . . or about men's health issues . . . or about natural food." The roster that lists editors and other contact information is usually on page two. Enter that information into your contact data base as soon as you can.

To know more about the reviewers or reporters who review for that magazine or newspaper, you need to go beyond the roster, directory, or masthead. Find the names of feature writers, reporters, and editors in the bylines (the tags that sometimes appear above a review and below the headline that tell who wrote the review). You also find them in credit lines (the little informationals at the end of the review that gives the name of the reviewer and perhaps her e-mail address). In either case, make a note of them in your database. A college group I belonged to runs a regular section in their quarterly titled "From the Pens." Record the titles of those book-related (or topic-related) features, too. You then mention them in your query letter so *they* know that *you* know who they are and what they do.

> **Tip:** Don't forget to include—and categorize—your online contacts. Bloggers, Web site owners (or reporters) who specialize in the topic of your book, even the large online news entities like *Newsweek*, *Huffington Post*, and *Politico*. They are not bound by space limitations like print media (no expensive paper and mailing!) and may have more varied departments that are a fit for your list. An example: authors of books on business should include any media that includes business news of any kind—and most do.

Your reviewer list should include the kind of media that publishes reviews we've talked about before. They are an integral part of the publishing industry. They include journals and other periodicals like *Kirkus*, *Booklist*, *Publishers Weekly*. You'll find a list of these reviewer journals on my Web site as well as online review sites and reviewers who do not discriminate against indie authors or publishers at bit.ly/GetEthicalReviews. Because you hold this book in your hands, you are now informed enough to have a good chance of getting reviews in them.

Review resources are everywhere. Nikki Leigh (nikki@nikkileigh.com) has a service to try if you are short on time. She supplies lists of Amazon reviewers who have reviewed comparable books to yours. Twitter has a list-making feature where you can classify your followers who review or blog on topics related to your book as you run across them.

ORGANIZING YOUR REVIEWER LISTS

Organizing a review list is a lot more important than it is to neaten up your work bench or sewing kit. It's how you can be sure your list of reviewers will be available whenever you need it, that you will be able to decipher it, and that you won't bother your contacts with messages they can't possibly use.

At first I made all kinds of separate lists in different categories including reviewers in Word. If I had known the power of Excel and similar programs way back then, I probably would have consolidated all of my lists in this single program. Now I have quite a mishmash. If you can start with one of these programs or know how to import your lists to it, now is the time before your list gets too long or you forget some of the details that will be helpful later.

When you put all your lists into one Excel-type file, categorize them by assigning codes to them so they can be pulled from the file separately as needed. My codes include NAT for national media; LOC for local; LIB for libraries; BKST for bookstores; CAT for catalogs; BLOG for bloggers; and, of course BIG REV for the prestigious, sought-after journals (the ones with firm deadlines and submission guidelines); and RDR REV for readers, bloggers, and others who are more interested in the content of a book than the press it's printed on or the year of copyright. I also use several other codes that work for the different kinds of books I write including WRT for media with an audience of writers. If you write political books or foody books or books about most anything else, you will need some super defined categories, too.

> **Tip:** Code or make a note in your contact file of those reviewers who accepted your book for review. You'll be glad you did when your next book comes out because you can specifically mention that they reviewed your work before. You may not be thinking about it now, but there is almost certain to be another book in your future.

But what about entries that cross over into two or more categories? Sometimes bloggers review. Sometimes they interview. Sometimes they want submissions for how-to articles to use as guest posts. That's when you'll end up with more than one code in the category column of your Excel file. Some of my bloggers get categorized three or four different ways. You can also assign a separate column to each category. Excel offers enough features to handle a very large assortment of people with specialties that can make a difference for your book.

I also make notes that help me address an editor in a more personal way. (Sally has two children, Josh and Sam." Or "Wanda is the author of *The Lilac Princess.*") If the entry is for a media outlet rather than an individual, the note might give me the name of a humor column or section of the newspaper that would be an especially suitable target for the topic of one of my books.

A properly coded list lets you use your filter function and e-mail merge function to target specific groups without bothering others on your list with unrelated messages. You can use codes to send out your media kit, invitations, media releases, query letters, and anything you are self-syndicating like columns or articles.

> **Hint:** New authors may have trouble accepting the idea that information they disseminate won't always be only about their books or be places we commonly think of for reviews. Some will be about the reviewing interests of the reviewer or how your book fits into the current news cycle. *Time* magazine still runs book reviews in their entertainment section and Fareed Zakaria features a book related to world affairs every week on his CNN Sunday morning show called *GPS*. You can even use codes for personal Christmas and holiday cards for publishing contacts. Because my poetry book celebrates Earth Day, I have a code (SP for *Sublime Planet*) so I can access anyone who is professionally or personally involved in environmental issues.

When you send book editors and reviewers information that fits their needs, you build credibility. When you send what appears to them to be unrelated to their audience, you lose it. Editors and reviewers open mail they are certain will benefit them.

> **Note:** This book is about reviews, so if you need more information on media releases (less accurately called press releases), media kits, and other aspects of marketing your book, you'll find that in the second edition of my multi award-winning *The Frugal Book Promoter* (bit.ly/FrugalBookPromo).

EXPANDING YOUR REVIEW LIST

Assembling your list of reviewers doesn't sound like much fun, but you will warm up to it when you see how it helps with your launch and most every promotion you undertake from this moment on. Now is the time to build your list with the names of reviewers you know, the ones you know of, and the ones you hope to get to know very soon.

Obviously this is where that categorizing and note-making becomes especially important. As an example, if you travel for the launch of your books, find local newspapers for reviews and other media for other kinds of promotion. A newspaper that reports on your book tour in their town may be ripe for a feature story or review. That contact may also share others in the media who can broaden your exposure for reviews placed in national or international publications now, later . . . or much later when your next book is released.

There are 350 million magazines published in the United States each year. Some of them are bound to be interested in what you write. You can find sources—newspapers, dailies, weeklies, TV, and radio stations—at Newslink.org and USNPL.com. Once a long time ago almost all media featured books. It is more difficult now and takes more research to find the ones that do. During your research, think creatively; when a newspaper or radio station doesn't have a regular feature that focuses on books, try to find a way around that. Your town's newspaper editor may be interested just because a local resident—you—has published. Trade papers and journals may be interested because the content of your book would serve their readers well.

One of my favorite resources has always been *Bacon's Directories*. It is now Cision (cision.com), an integrated platform. These huge reference books were too expensive for most authors or even small publishing companies to buy, so this online access to TV, radio, newspapers, etc. is welcome. I especially like it for getting regional publicity for an event when I am promoting at an out-of-town venue.

Tip: You won't at first know these out-of-town contacts—or some local ones for that matter. Do not assume that is a barrier to a broader relationship. They are people, after all. Find ways to keep in touch with them, beginning with writing thank-you notes to those who request review copies of your books—both at the time you send your book and after the review is published. Find legitimate ways to stay in touch with them beyond that, too. If they get a promotion or write an article you find provocative, congratulations may be called for. Or you can suggest they review a book you have read that might be right for their readership. That's two people you've connected with—the author and the reviewer—two people who have even more reason to remember you next time you contact them.

Join a forum or list-serve (like those at Yahoogroups.com) where people interested in the subject of your nonfiction or the theme of your fiction gather to share and chat. After you've been around a while, ask them for a review. Many will be delighted to get a free copy of your book and, because they know you, they may give your book more effusive praise than you'd ever hoped for.

Did you know that Amazon.com gives authors and reviewers links to a dedicated profile page? You can easily find "Top Reviewers" by clicking on the byline links of each reviewer you find who seems compatible with your book. Top Amazon reviewers are marked as such but some who haven't worked their way to the top may be more accessible. You may find an e-mail address or Web site on the reviewer's page that puts you in direct contact. If not, a search engine can help. Be sure to only add reviewers to your list who have an interest in your genre or topic, and tailor your query letter so he or she can tell you have done your homework.

Once your book is published, start collecting a list of readers or fans who write to you, meet you at events, meet you on social media, etc. Some of these people will be pleased to add a review to an online bookstore like Amazon though most won't think of it on their own. You can ask some personally or you can put out a general call on one of these networks. Goodreads.com has a contest feature where you offer a certain number of review copies in exchange for a review.

Assemble all of the lists I've mentioned the moment the idea of a book enters your head. Record names, e-mails, and addresses (for postcards and invitations to launches) of anyone you meet. Don't overlook your holiday card list, lists from club rosters, social groups, and your mother's bridge club list. You'll use them for your book launch and forever after.

> **Note:** "Forever after" now applies to books because the Web and digital publishing have made it easy to print a book on demand, and because Amazon.com keeps out-of-print books alive with their New and Used feature. Other than the very few books that become classics, "forever after" is something new in the world of publishing and is very good news for authors no matter what kind of press they are published on.

WHAT IS THE BEST WAY TO REACH REVIEWERS ON YOUR LIST?

I'm glad you asked. The answer varies depending on the contact, but generally I love e-mail for getting reviews because e-mail is the most frugal way to disseminate most any information or request. Here are some helps for sending e-mail to reviewers or about anyone else:

- In general, authors tend to get better results if their e-requests appear to come from their own little selves. Here's how to do that:
  - Use warm or slightly colloquial language when you approach individual reviewers. Write all queries in first person (yes, your request for a review is still a query), but the tone can vary depending on how familiar you are with the recipients.
  - You can use blind addresses when you send under ten. Otherwise avoid them because, as Victor Volkman, publisher of Loving Hearts Press says, "too many blind addresses are a flag to spam catching tools." The only address that should show is your own.
  - E-mail services like MailChimp can be expensive but might have the odor of commercial and uncaring. If "commercial" doesn't fit your image, Volkman says "avoid their fancy-pants templates to make your request look like regular e-mail."
  - Include your book cover image, your headshot, or your logo in your automated e-mail signature.
  - As a courtesy, include an unsubscribe message at the end of your message, but make that warm, too. "If you don't care to receive my very occasional e-mails about all-things-writing, just let me know by sending a reply to this e-mail."
- You have control of your lists and the e-mails you send. In an article for IBPA (Independent Book

Publishers Association) magazine, Kimberly Grabas says, "Twitter, Facebook, Pinterest, Instagram, LinkedIn . . . decide how you communicate, who gets to see your content, or whether you get to be a part of the conversation at all (break the rules and you're out, with no way to contact your followers)." Her comment underscores the importance of keeping your own lists apart from whatever you're doing on other platforms. Kimberly is the founder of YourWriterPlatform.com.

- Services like gmail.com and aol.com keep excellent records of the addresses and the dates of your mail.
- E-mail encourages a two-way conversation. Your contact(s) can easily ask questions. Do *not* use a "no-reply" function that some services prefer.

> **Exception:** I prefer real paper stationery for thank-you notes that go to reviewers.

The people who respond to your query can easily become your "Top 50 Reviewers" or "Top 100 Networkers." All it takes is a moment to add another code by their name on that Excel file you are building (or start to a new list). These names are valuable for all kinds of marketing needs, but in terms of reviews, you'll love having it when you release your next book, your next promotional e-book, or any other marketing you do.

PLANNING FOR PREORDERS

You might have guessed from the prefix ("pre") in "preorders," that you must think about them long before your book's launch date. It is important that your online bookstore buy page looks as if it has been given some tender loving care during this prerelease period including a good start on reader reviews.

Amazon recently announced a program that lets self-published authors offer preorders to their readers. Big publishers have used preorders to boot up sales and create a buzz for some time. Self-published or traditionally published authors can now put a preorder program in place on their e-book pages to help promote the launch of their e-books on Amazon (but not their paperbacks—yet). Go to your KDP (Kindle Direct Publishing) account to set up your new book for preorders.

Amazon says,

> "We're excited to announce that you can now make your new books available for preorder in Kindle Stores worldwide. With a few quick and easy steps you can create a preorder page up to nine days in advance of your book's release date—your preorder product page will be created within twenty-four hours. When you make your book available for preorder, customers can order the book anytime leading up to the release date you set. We will deliver it to them on that date.

> "One advantage of using [our preorder benefit] is that you can start promoting your Kindle book preorder page on Author Connect, Goodreads, your personal Web site, and other places ahead of its release to help

build excitement for your book. Preorders contribute toward sales rank and other Kindle Store merchandising ahead of release."

Just in case you are worried about planning a promotion that is available only to Kindle readers, don't be. Readers needn't own a Kindle reader to read your book. When they buy from Kindle, they are offered a free Kindle app that lets them download a PDF file to your computer or a specially formatted copy of your book for any other device they may own.

Tip: Do not be tempted to forego this preorder marketing tool unless you have already missed your opening for this important opportunity. Alas, the only alternative to the presales promotion is to work your little fanny off on your marketing plan to try to make up for the loss. How to put double steam behind the review-getting basics is up next in Chapter Six.

This Kindle preorder program makes it all the more important for you to have reviews on your Kindle buy page early on—even if you don't publish your paperback until later. You don't want any buy page—ever—to look lonely and forgotten. You want this first introduction to your book to be just as professional as the book you just wrote and edited.

Note: If your Kindle page and the buy page for your paper book aren't linked to one another, go to the contact function in Amazon's Author Connect and ask Amazon worker bees to do it for you.

I refined my publishing process over the years. I did it mostly because of benefits like this preorder program and the app that lets Kindle readers choose delivery in a format that fits their e-reader devices or a PDF for reading on their computers once they've clicked on the "buy" button. I don't use my valuable writing time to format and install my e-books across several different platforms. This single adjustment saves me hours of time tracking sales and payments, too. It just isn't worth it to me not to direct all my traffic to Amazon because I get these benefits at no charge; it saves me time uploading my books, and offers other promotions and exposure. And, no, I don't get any affiliate money for telling you that.

Tip: As I suggest elsewhere in this book, I use the Twitter and other social networking icons that appear on my Amazon buy pages to let Amazon "make" tweets for me. By doing so, Amazon's algorithms get pinged and, as nearly as I can tell, those algorithms don't much care that it's me—the author—using this fancy tool. It's a handy way to spread the word about preorders.

Okay, next up. Let's talk about the tools you need to reach out and *get* those reviews.

Section III
Your Review-Getting Arsenal

"Authors who don't know the basics of PR are likely to run into some great big concrete K road barriers when they try to get reviews." ~ CHJ

I know many authors raised up with the traditional ideas of the publishing world would prefer to avoid anything that resembles marketing, but having the basics under their belts makes their hunt for reviews easier. The author who develops a knack for writing a great query letter gets more positive responses from more influential reviewers with less effort.

I wish all authors knew—deep down in their bones—that marketing tools are the magic that makes bestsellers. Someone—author, publicist, or publisher—must have the knowledge and the motivation necessary to propel a book to stardom. Think of the getting-reviews process as an art of its own, one that must be learned or at least remolded to the needs of the publishing industry.

Chapter Six
Magic Bullets for Getting Reviews

"Getting reviews isn't magic. What's magic is having enough knowledge about the process to be confident. " ~ CHJ

Most authors want their books to be reviewed, but many are scared spitless of what those reviews might say. Byron once asked his publisher to "send me no more reviews of any kind." He thought Keats had been killed by one bad review (which, we know, in retrospect, was not true).

Some writers—particularly those who have made it to bestseller lists—believe that reviews were responsible for their success; many others have been successful without them or in spite of them.

What can't be argued is that librarians and bookstore buyers peruse *The Library Journal* and other major review journals, book review sections, as well as media material the major publishers send to them. Most authors would like to see their books in libraries and on bookstore shelves and good reviews are the fast lanes to those shelves—sometimes the only lanes.

The good news is that we live in a time—the best time I think—when we have control of our own writing careers and the success of our books. Even when we screw up, we can backtrack, learn more, and reinvent our attack.

The only constraint to these amazing times—I prefer to think of them as benefits—is that we must learn how to take control of the process. That requires knowing our industry and knowing the specific marketing skills that keep its little engines humming.

WRITING QUERY LETTERS IS NOT DIFFICULT

"Not difficult" is one thing, but writing query letters that work is magic—and absolutely essential once we're beyond our first efforts at getting Mom or Sis to write reviews for us. In fact it is so essential, I dedicate Chapter Seven to the art of the query letter.

Still we need to talk about it as a review-getting magic-bullet and this chapter is an overview of those bullets. We need that overview because we think (or fervently hope!) we can avoid all that marketing we never intended to learn when we began to write a book. But here's the thing. No matter how much we love our relatives' reviews, it won't be long before we realize we don't have enough relatives to sustain a great review campaign and that the ones they write don't have the impact of a review from an unbiased stranger, an expert reviewer, or a credible expert. To get those kinds of reviews, you'll have to learn to write a query letter.

The great news is that your query letter is the perfect tool for getting a lot of attention for your book beyond getting reviews. The less-welcome news is that a query letter isn't exactly like writing to an aunt in Florida. Put simply, without the fundamentals the industry expects, your letter won't do what it needs to do—that is, get reviews for your book.

Though this may seem a bit backwards, let's pretend for now that you have read Chapter Seven and have a query letter template ready to go and all you have to do is tweak it a bit each time you approach a reviewer. We'll talk about the tweaking process later, too.

Dreaming of big-journal reviews is only natural, and authors in-the-know start preparing for this magic bullet first. Trouble is, it can be tough to get them—especially for self- and partner-published authors. These journals have tons of preferences, guidelines, and rules you must follow. If you have your heart set on seeing your book in lots of bookstores and libraries and if you haven't missed their deadlines *and* if you have your query letter template ready in time, shooting for these stars may be worth the trouble.

Big journals are only one of the major categories where readers and influentials in the publishing industry will see reviews of your book. Others are:

- Big city newspaper/book section reviews.
- Blogs, online review sites, and local newspaper reviews.
- Social network reviews. (Goodreads and even networks not known for reviews. I mean, a nice endorsement or micro review on Facebook or Twitter can't hurt!)
- Reader reviews on the buy pages of online bookstores like Barnes & Noble (BN.com), Amazon.com, and even indie bookstores that also sell online like Powell's (powells.com).

My point is that you have choices. Evaluate what is important to you in terms of your dreams, your chances of getting reviews in each category, and the time you must spend to query for those reviews and make them part of your overall marketing campaign. Books that have been ignored by *The New York Times* have become bestsellers; others that received rave reviews never made it to that same publication's bestseller list. It is all a game. We can choose not to play, but if we don't play, we'll never know if we could have won. We'll start with the basics for the big journals first because once mastered, they can be applied to any (or all) of the review paths you choose.

ADVANCE PLANNING

Advance planning is one of the most ignored bullets in your review-getting six shooter. You need to give yourself the time to know the rules—especially the big journals' be-on-time rule—and abide by them.

You also need to be very, very lucky—or know what some now call a legitimate hack for getting reviews. I hate the term "hack," because it smacks of illegal and devious. Notice I put "legitimate" before "hack." But "hack" also induces visions of high tech interference and the ones I share with you are definitely not high tech.

More on those . . . ahem, "hacks" later in the "All Is Not Lost" section of this chapter. Right now let's talk about that often-ignored advance planning thing.

Here are a few of those all-important advance planning musts:

- When you sign your contract with a publisher, negotiate. You want advance review copies of your book sent to the major journals before their *twelve-to-sixteen-week deadline*, preferably at no cost to you. Big influencers in the publishing world pay more attention to a query or a review copy that comes directly from a publisher's marketing department. Even more than one that comes from a professional publicist.
- If you are unable to get your publisher to agree to send review copies to reviewers they find for you *and* the ones who have accepted queries from you, try to negotiate a lower price for review copies you buy from them, preferably at their cost which is less than the 40% or even 60% discount they offer you for other copies you buy directly from them.

Note: You should also ask for assurance that they will give you the list of review journals they plan to submit to so you don't duplicate their efforts. That way you can expand on it with confidence that you aren't spending precious marketing dollars unnecessarily.

If your negotiating efforts fail, it is time to either choose another publisher (if you can) or to take matters into your own hands:

- Use prepublish time to find the contact information of review journals and major magazines and newspapers that feature book sections. There is more on that process and more resources for you at this page in the Writers Resources section of my Web site (HowToDoItFrugally.com).
- If your publisher will not have your book ready for release before that sixteen-week cutoff date, self-publish your own advance review or readers' copies (also called ARCs) and distribute them yourself. I tell you how to do that to avoid unnecessary expense and fatal mistakes in the "All Is Not Lost" section of this chapter. Most publishers own the rights to your book during the entire term of your contract, so check your contract to be sure you can do it within legal boundaries and, if not, negotiate for permission. Point out how they will benefit from your partnership in this effort.

   Caveat: Distribute your own ARCs only if you are willing to risk the expense for limited results, and if you are willing to take the pains to do it according to firm and fast industry rules outlined in Chapter Eight on sending your books to reviewers.

YOUR MEDIA LISTS ARE LARGE-CALIBER BULLETS

The big journals on your reviewer list need heavy ammunition and an early bird sensibility because they require a fourteen-to-sixteen week lead. Here are some of the major reviewers to aim at:

- *Booklist* at the American Library Association (ala.org/booklist).
- *Entertainment Weekly Magazine* (ew.com/).
- *Kirkus Reviews* (kirkusreviews.com/).
- *Library Journal* (libraryjournal.com/).
- *The New York Times Book Review* (nytimes.com/).
- *Los Angeles Times Book Review* (latimes.com/).
- *Chicago Tribune Books* (chicagotribune.com/).
- *American Book Review,* Illinois State University.
- *Small Press Review.* Poetry and fiction only (dustbooks.com/).
- *Publishers Weekly* (publishersweekly.com/).
- *Amazon.com,* Editorial, 520 Pike St., Suite 1800, Seattle, WA 98101.
- *Book Page* (bookpage.com/). Submissions needn't be brand new titles.
- Trade magazines associated with an industry related to the topic of your book. Use Cision.com (formerly *Bacon's Directories*) at the reference desk of your library to find them.

- The book or arts and entertainment section of your nearest metropolitan newspaper. Find a list of other major newspapers and other review aids on my Web site's Writers' Resources page for reviews (bit.ly/NewspaperRvwList).

  Note: In an earlier chapter, I mention that *Kirkus, Publishers Weekly,* and others have paid-for review services. Offering this service is a way for publishers to affect another income stream at a time when profits are not as great as they once were. You also may recall that I don't recommend using them. Bookstore buyers, book editors, and other publishing experts know the difference between journalistically legitimate reviews and those authors pay for. If you are tempted, keep in mind that many of these same journals make it clear (through the formatting or design of the magazine) which reviews are chosen editorially for a review and which are paid for, thus relegating independently-published or paid-for review to the status of second-class citizenry.

That sixteen week deadline for submissions to these journals comes fast (and goes fast, too!). The beauty is that you can make lists and prepare query letters before your book is published.

Some review journals welcome indie publishers, and more are accepting them all the time. Some say they don't consider independent (self-published titles), but everyone knows they make exceptions. Those privileged authors feel it was worth sending an ARC and query letter so professionally wrought that gatekeepers couldn't ascertain it didn't come from the most respected publisher or publicist. Those who have no success usually wish they hadn't wasted their time.

The following review journals are amenable to reviewing alternative forms of publishing. They are growing in status with each passing day and some have more lax deadlines so I include them as viable possibilities for your big journal quest. Though they do not discriminate against books published by small presses or by the author him- or herself, no reviewer, review journal, or site guarantees a review for all submissions:

- *Independent Publisher* (independentpublisher.com/).
- *Midwest Book Review* (midwestbookreview.com/get_rev.htm).
- *Foreword Magazine* (forewordmagazine.com/) also offers contests that accept self-published books.
- Omnimystery (mysteriousreviews.com/mysterious-review.html).
- NPR Books (npr.org/books/).

Other aids include:

- Net Galley (netgalley.com) offers a review-getting service for authors for a fee. Discounts are available to members of Independent Book

Publishers Association (ibpa-online.org/) and that organization does accept individual authors as members.

- Literary Marketplace (literarymarketplace.com) has many helpful lists and services.

Find lists of review sites at:

- *The Indie View* (theindieview.com/).
- *EBook Crossroads* (ebookcrossroads.com/book-reviewsers.html).
- *Midwest Book Review* (midwestbookreview.com/links/other_rev.htm).
- The review page on the Writers Resources section of my Web site (bit.ly/GetEthicalReviews).

> **Note**: When you submit galleys or self-published ARCs, some journals ask you to send a final copy of your book when it is finished as proof that it was released.

Here are other respected online review sites you can query. They post the request to a bulletin that goes out to their stable of reviewers asking for a volunteer to read your book. If no reviewer volunteers, you will not be reviewed.

For starters try:

- CompulsiveReader.com.
- BookPleasures.com.
- MyShelf.com.
- ReaderViews.com.

The lists I've given you are compiled for the frugal author who must work on a postage and free-book budget. None guarantee a free review, but all subscribe to my no #bookbigotry policy. If your budget allows, a Google search will give you enough resources to expand them a thousand fold.

Caveat: Because addresses and submission guidelines change frequently, check for current particulars. You will also benefit by knowing (and spelling correctly) the names of the editors or reviewers you send your query to and knowing what genres they prefer. Because personnel change frequently, knowing these names requires a recent visit to that review outlet's Web site.

Frugal Hint: When you ask for reviews, send a book or ARC with your query only when submission guidelines ask for you to do so. For all others, wait to send your ARC until reviewers indicate an interest in your book based on the query letter you sent to them. Know that media personnel and many universities and other government-related offices often have policies in place for their e-mail service to reject mail with attachments because they don't want to risk viruses from unknown sources.

ALL IS NOT LOST

If you miss the deadline for the biggies or you prefer to spend your valuable time on methods that are more likely to result in acceptance, there are other review avenues to pursue. They may be just as effective—especially if getting readership for your book is more important to you than bookstore exposure (which rarely results in the massive readership authors think it will).

Legitimate hacks and back doors are magic bullets for the author who didn't know the big-review journals' rules early enough. They don't sound ethical, but they are legitimate techniques that help authors get exposure when they miss deadlines. In fact they work any old time—now or long after your book's release.

Go in the back door of media that have audiences that would be interested in your book. You do that by reading reviews in journals and online to find reviewers who write columns or frequently write reviews or cover news stories of books in your genre. You get their names from a search engine and their bylines or the little credits that get printed at the ends of lots of reviews (especially reviews written by freelancers). You then contact these columnists and reviewers *directly* rather than going through the media's editorial process. When you send them a query, mention the review you saw and where you found it. This works especially well for industry favorites like *Booklist* and *Library Journal*. I know it does because it worked for my first novel.

> **Hint:** I'm thinking of publishing a couple of chapters of my next novel—sort of a combination ARC and chapbook—to send to a long list of booksellers and reviewers (including some of my back-door sources). The booklet would include necessary disclaimers and metadata—those pieces of information that would

normally be included in a sell sheet. (Search the entries for "metadata" in the Index of this book for lists of what information gets included in a sell sheet.) I would mail it along with a cover letter suggesting we plan well ahead for a reading, workshop, interview or review so I have time to promote it well. In the query I'd make it clear that I would be pleased to send the finished book once it is available. This booklet will be more expensive than using e-mail, but having a tangible sample of my writing—one with a higher perceived value than a query letter on its own—will reap better results. In retailing, we call that "perceived value."

Here's the important thing, though. Even if you hit the jackpot and get reviews in several of the big journals, that doesn't mean you should rest on your laurels. These alternative review possibilities are well worth going after now and later—in conjunction with the big guys or on their own.

Online blog tours are relatively easy and inexpensive compared to old fashioned book tours. Online tours compress appearances similar to real-life venues into a short period of time with no transportation costs. Traditionally published and independent authors can reach hundreds of thousands and maybe millions of readers with comparatively little work.

Stephanie Meyer of *Twilight* fame showed us all how effective blogs are for targeting an audience. Her blog tour plan was such a marketing coup it was featured on the front page of the business section of the *Los Angeles Times*.

It seems that though her much-respected publisher had provided her with a Web site, she felt it didn't fully reflect the themes she preferred to highlight so she opened an independent site that focused on the branding she preferred. She then approached bloggers with a history of reviewing or discussing young adult novels or that showed a preference for books that dealt with vampires and Christian-leaning content. Many of these blogs were run by young people themselves.

She didn't construct an actual blog tour as it came to be known, but she put in place the most important essentials. She built relationships with each of her chosen bloggers. She frequented their blogs. She commented—broadened the discussion—on others' posts. She judiciously dropped in information (complete with a link to her site) about her *Twilight* books. After an . . . er, suitable amount of time . . . she pitched her bloggers with the idea of a review—and later an interview—and supplied a book to the takers. Soon her books had soared to bestseller status. In other words, she respectfully contributed in ways that added value. The rest (including her movie series) is history.

Note: Authors—especially fiction writers—often make the mistake of assuming that exposure must always be about their books. This single article in the *LA Times* featuring Stephanie's alternative marketing plan may have garnered her more attention (and book sales) than a good portion of the attention she received from blogs dedicated to young adult books. She or her publicist may have pitched this feature story idea using a simple query letter to newspaper business sections to snag this marketing coup.

Besides the "relationship-intrigue model" that Meyers set up with her bloggers, a more elaborate tour might include contests, prizes, a directory with links and dates of blog tour appearances set up on a Web site so fans can follow them all. It would have an opt-in function so that the process collects names of participating fans. Opt-in features like this grow the author's reach for future promotions. The prizes might be extravagant—a collection of gifts that must be shipped—or an assortment of e-gifts (like stories or e-books donated by other authors who write in the same or similar genres). These fellow authors' generosity becomes an outreach to more readers because they—in turn—run blogs or invitations in their newsletters to visit the blog tour page and enter the contest. Sometimes a whole battery of e-prizes is offered to anyone who clicks through with the purchase of a book. About those generous fellow authors? They get exposure with book cover and headshot images and short synopses or pitches for their books!

You can borrow Meyers' original, simple model, do a full blog tour on your own, or hire an expert to help you with it. Grassroots marketing has always worked. It's personal and caring and so encourages loyalty. I prefer the term "grassroots" over the "million eyeballs" term bandied about these days, which doesn't pretend to be grassroots or personal. You will have to figure out who your real audience is and spend time researching exactly where they hang out. Persistence counts, too.

Blog tours have become so effective that some have begun to offer blog tour services. Nikki Leigh (nikki@nikkileigh.com) is one of my favorite blog-tour planners and it's one of the few services offered to authors that I think is worth the money because:

- You avoid making mistakes.
- You benefit from their Rolodex of people who own blogs related to the topic of your book, and you can add your own list to their list of bloggers to make the tour more effective.
- Many of the bloggers your blog tour service works with (if not all) review your book, accept an article from you complete with byline and credit, or interview you—anything that works for both you and your blogger-host. Each one becomes part of your now-and-ever-after list of reviewers or next-time blog hosts.
- Bloggers who are new to you are usually happy to give you the rights to reuse their reviews as long as you credit them with their bylines, bios, and links (URLs) to their blogs.
- The links to a specific blog post are often permalinks, which means they access your specific blog post indefinitely. That means you can feel comfortable linking to the post for a whole multitude of your marketing needs.
- You learn the hard-won secrets of these experts so you can reuse them again on your own—for this book or your next. Some blog tour operators include an e-mail blast that can push the e-edition of your book to number-one status in its category

on Amazon. If (when?) your book achieves that status, you can market it with something like, "An Amazon #1 Bestseller Editing Book" as a motto or in tweets.

Occasions for an additional tour might be:

- When you publish the e-book version of your book some weeks after the launch of the paperback.
- When you publish an audio of your book.
- Maybe years later when you publish a second edition.
- When you publish your next book or your work appears in an anthology.
- When you publish the next book in your series.
- When you publish a boxed set of your series.
- To celebrate an award your book receives.
- When your book sales have slowed.

Just think, with each of these tours, you will add new reviewers to your growing cadre of willing (and future!) reviewers and when you decide to do another tour, it will be easier for you. You'll know some obscure ways to make Amazon's magic work harder for you. You'll have your query letter template ready to go (or ready to revise), and you'll have many other promotional devices in your bag of tricks that work well for blogs—like contest ideas, recycled or repurposed articles, and interviews.

A few more review-getting techniques are available for you to use for your book's release and other ongoing publicity. In fact, the review-getting process may be one of the most flexible tools in your book marketing kit—the tool you lean on most as your writing career advances. Here are a few we haven't yet discussed:

- To get more reader reviews (and maybe others, too), put a suggestion for your readers to do so in the backmatter of your book. Author and book marketer R. J. Adams says, "If someone makes it to the back of the book, chances are they liked it. So you should take advantage of this opportunity to [engage readers] who probably liked your book." They are the same folks who keep your book active rather than dying the slow death most books experienced before the Web and online reviews existed.
- Don't overlook staff members at bookstores. A large percentage of the staffs at bookstores I frequent (and have presented at) are avid readers and many are fellow writers. Some do reviews for the bookstore's newsletter. Sometimes they hang brief reviews on the shelf where the book is displayed. All of them are influencers. Because they are all human, they love it when authors show their appreciation for what they do. Your personal thank-you gift to them should be a signed copy of your book.

  Tip: When I sign books at a bookstore, I pick out the staff member who seems most interested in my book and offer her a signed copy in exchange for posting a review on

Amazon or taping a mini review on the shelf where the bookstore lets my book camp out.

- Although I don't believe advertising is effective for authors who are on a budget or can't afford a campaign of frequent and targeted ads, you could try a few as a networking tool if you've had difficulty getting a Web site or newspaper to assign a reviewer to your book. It is a long shot because editorial departments should not be influenced by the advertising departments, but you may find that interest in reviewing your book increases after you've signed up for an ad.

- Independent Book Publishers of America (ibpa-online.org/) offers an advertising program that might prove effective for your book. Their members can access a pay-for cooperative ad on a full page in *Publishers Weekly.* There is an option (for an additional fee) to have your book's cover image included on the ad on the *cover* of the same issue. It is expensive. There is no guarantee that it will result in sales. It is an alternative that works if you are too late to qualify for a free review from *Publishers Weekly*, or if I have convinced you not to pay for a review from them (which can cost somewhere in the neighborhood of IBPA's ad offer and carries the distinct drawback of being a paid-for review).

Note: One major advantage of using this IBPA benefit: You can use "As Seen on the Cover of *Publishers Weekly*" forever after—on your business cards, your Web site, and about anywhere else you mention your book.

- Subscribe to online newsletters. As you read them, look for review resources. Sometimes the newsletter will print one of your existing reviews—free—or you can trade them an ad in their newsletter for one in yours.
- Ask for reviews using the special features or contests offered by Goodreads and Library Thing. If you choose to do this, limit the number of review copies you offer. You can always repeat the offer later, if you wish.
- Put out calls for reviews in your own newsletter. Your subscribers already know your work and are probably getting the benefit of your wisdom at no cost. They are likely to want to read your new book and happy to get a review copy at no charge.
- Call for reviews on the list-serves (Yahoogroups for like-minded people) you frequent, the forums you contribute to, and other groups you belong to, both online and off. The acceptance rate will usually be higher than some of your other review-getting efforts because people who know you are more inclined to want to read your book.
- Check for groups on social networks like Facebook (or start one) that swap reviews. Ted Farrar shares this on a LinkedIn chat: "There's an Author Review Swap on LinkedIn. We have a small but growing group of people who swap reviews. We keep it honest and simple: Post information on your book, request reviewers, then swap as many times as you

like." I can see how reviews obtained (and given) this way may not be as honest as we'd like, but this plan does seem a cut above paying for reviews as long as both parties in the trade have an interest in ethics and have discussed that the review may include criticism to increase the credibility of the reviews. You may find swap groups that make this clear in their mission statements or otherwise outline plans for addressing problems that may crop up.

- Melinda Brasher, a regular contributor to the WritersOnTheMove blog (writersonthemove.com/), suggests BlogTour.org for finding reviewers and interviewers. She says, "You can meet bloggers willing to do guest posts, publish excerpts, give interviews, and do reviews."
- Do a search for "reviewer" on Twitter. Add them to your Twitter list of reviewers for future use. Then use Direct Messaging and say something that lets the reviewer know you have been following them. Follow up with queries for reviews both before your book's launch and after when you seek to keep your sales soaring.
- Authors often forget to use their own contact lists to find reviewers. You have superfans hidden away in every contact list I mention in Chapter Five. Ask your other author and reading friends who know you well to recommend reviewers to you, too.
- Stephen H. Manchester, author of *The Rockin' Chair*, says, " . . . nothing can ever substitute for name dropping. When you receive a favorable review from someone who enjoyed your work, your

next question should be, 'Would you know of any other editors, authors, etc. who might also like my book and consider endorsing it [or writing a review]?' Being sent to a book reviewer/blogger by someone he/she personally knows nearly guarantees an [acceptance]."

- Publishers often ask their other authors to write reviews for the new book on the block. Many smaller presses don't think to do that, so it may be up to you to keep your publisher—big or little—on their toes. Or you can do it on your own. You will be more successful if you tell these sister and brother authors you will excerpt blurbs from their reviews and promote them with credits and links should they decide to support you.

  Caution: Be wary about using too many review excerpts from well-known authors published by the same press as your book. Jim Misko of Northwest Ventures Press in Anchorage, AK, says, "I'm not impressed with the blurbs given by authors of the same publishing house at the request of the editor. I doubt they even read the book." He says the average reader may not notice, but that it should be a consideration when your marketing is directed at gatekeepers in the publishing industry.

- Check to see if the blogs you are researching for your blog tour have blogrolls. Bloggers often use blogrolls to refer their visitors to other blogs—sort of recommendations to blogs with a similar focus.

- Most authors forget to send queries to the magazines published by different departments at the university they attended and the magazines published by the organizations they belonged to in college. These publications may be as interested in a feature story as in reviewing your book.

  Note: In these cases, individual requests—really your query letter disguised as a personal letter but tailored to the interests of the prospective reviewer—almost always work better than a formal query letter.

- Nonfiction writers often forget to query trade magazines and Web sites related to their topics for reviews. Ditto for related organizations that publish Web sites, newsletters, or magazines for their membership such as AAA Auto Club.
- We tend to think of book clubs as a way to reach readers after a book has been released, but book clubs may be interested in reading and reviewing your book before the release. Think of such an event as a prepublish promotion or a way to get advance reader reviews. Think of them as a whole cartridge of marketing bullets for before, after, and ever-after. Most clubs have never been approached with a prepublish query, so you must be prepared to suggest how much fun it can be and how neat it would be for them to have what is essentially a limited edition ARC or prepublished copy of your book.

Note: In your pitch suggest that a review on their blog or on an online bookstore would be a gift to you and to the publishing industry that provides them with so much pleasure.

- Here are some places you might find reading groups or clubs—you know—the old-fashioned get-together kinds of groups where you can also develop a face-to-face network with readers:
  o Your work place. Check the bulletin board and company newsletter. Talk to your fellow workers about a free book in trade for a review even if you find no reading groups there.
  o Synagogues, mosques, and church groups.
  o Service and social groups and organizations.
  o Bookstores. Some bookstores have reading groups planned and executed by volunteer readers.
  o Libraries and museums, both public and private.
  o School and parent groups.
  o Lists in newspaper and magazine calendar sections.
  o For online groups, use search engines. My search on "reading groups" reaped resources in the millions including organizations that sponsor reading groups in specific genres like mystery readers.
- When you print special editions of your book to be used as ARCs, tactfully suggest a review in the disclaimer. "This is an Advance Reader/Reviewer

Copy offered to those who agree to review [this book] or offer an endorsement of it for publication." Don't forget to include contact information for those who want to partner with you as a result of your call-to-arms.

- When you send free books to influencers in the industry, tuck in a little invitation or suggestion that an unbiased review would be appreciated.

About that last bullet: Judith Briles, a multi award-winning author of several books (including how-to books for writers), slipped a straight-forward request into a book I received from her. It went like this:

"Thank you for buying *Author YOU: Creating and Building Your Author and Book Platforms* (bit.ly/AuthorYou). Here's another amazing gift for my amazing publishing friends, too. It is redesigned for authoring and publishing. And . . . please, please go to Amazon.com and post a fabulous review on the *Author YOU* book . . . . It's very important to do this to support the book—and me—in the Amazon world. Judith."

A direct request like this works well because it combines passion and generosity and sets an example of great marketing for her reading audience.

The note you include in your complimentary books might read:

"My first novel [your title here] is finally here. I've been dreaming of doing this for a lifetime. I need your help to make it available to others who will enjoy it. Please go to my book's page at [the shortened or embedded URL for your book's buy page here]. Scroll down to find the link where you can add a review and tell your fellow readers at bit about the book. It's a way to support the publishing world and my dream! This book comes to you with my love, [Your name here.]

To find even more reviewers, you can put your reporter's hat on and ask—tactfully—for what you need. Make the point that a review is a gift to you, a gift that authors treasure above all others—whether it comes from a reviewer or a reader. Try some of these possibilities:

- Ask fellow attendees at writers' conferences.
- Ask directors of writers' conferences if they offer a review exchange or have other suggestions for you.
- Ask writing instructors if they have a list of reviewers or know where you can find one.
- When you're on the Web, look at the resource pages of the Web sites owned by how-to authors of books for writers and of online book review sites.
- Think about classes you have taken. The instructors may have a policy against reviewing students' work, but your fellow students may review yours. (I hope you would try to do the same for them!)
- Ask members of your critique group.
- Ask members of the organizations you belong to. Writing organizations come to mind, but members

of other organizations may be even more open to your suggestion. It may be something they've never done, may never have thought about doing, and they may find it is lots of fun.

- When you read, make a note of reviews and the names of those who wrote them that you find in some issues of magazines like *Time* and newspapers around the world.

The advantages of alternative review-getting methods include:

- It may be easier to build relationships with those you contact who aren't accustomed to getting requests for reviews every day. That can lead to even more publicity—like an interview or publication of an excerpt—for your book and for your next book.
- Most alternative reviewers do not have deadlines or limit reviews by copyright year.
- Many alternative outlets accept reader reviews, and many readers are elated to be asked to share their opinions with others.
- These alternative sources—online or in print—often include links to your Web site, your own blog, and your online sales page. Click-and-buy is an easier sale than delayed purchases produced by print journals.
- Many of these sources want you to send them the digital file for your book rather than a paperback by post. That is, of course, less costly. They may use different terms for the digital file: E-book, e-galley,

PDF file—even Kindle. If they don't specify, ask them what they prefer.

> **Warning:** In case you missed my last warning, sending an electronic copy of your book attached to an e-mail query seems like a time saver, but don't. Many reviewers won't open e-mail communications with attachments so your query may not get read. Offer to send an electronic copy in another e-mail or a hardcopy by post. Please *don't* try to convince reviewers to accept the e-copy over the paperback. It's insensitive; if they accept your book, they should be able to read it in whatever form they prefer.

I know. You're saying, "so enough! How do I *get started?*" I want you to do that with not just a great query letter, but a query letter a cut above great! Stay for the next chapter for query letter advice you probably have seen nowhere else.

Chapter Seven

The Cut-Above Query Letter Process

"No matter how an author chooses to publish, it behooves her to be familiar with all the marketing tools. Here's the joyful news: To get reviews, an author only needs a few of the basics." ~ CHJ

Your query letter is as close to a magic bullet as you can get for getting the reviews that count most for your book. A professional query letter makes professional reviewers who write for major review journals and newspaper book sections sit up and take notice.

Gatekeepers—folks like reviewers, editors, and bloggers— usually learn about you when they open a letter or e-mail with your query or cover letter in it. If you are not known to them, it is the first (and probably the only) thing they have to judge you and your book.

Note: I've mentioned before that you shouldn't send attachments with your e-mail. Many organizations and people who work with the public don't open mail that has an attachment icon because they fear viruses. Some have servers that block those mails entirely. Instead, offer to send additional material like your media kit that gives your contacts all the information and tools they need to help you by attachment upon request or by USPS (United States Postal Service). That these gatekeepers—specifically those located in government, academic, or large corporate offices— often block e-mail with attachments is a good reason to choose USPS as your first means to contact them. That way, you can send a packet that includes query letter, media kit, and even a book or galley—all spruced up in a free priority mailer provide by carriers like USPS or FedEx. Even then the heavy load of getting your contact to pay attention to the whole presentation is carried by your query letter.

For an author seeking reviews, there is little difference between a cover letter and a query letter. A *query* letter asks or tells the person it addresses what the author of the letter needs. A *cover* is an introduction to what is being presented in the package. It may not ask for something specific, though it, too, benefits if you indicate your reasons for sending it. When requesting reviews by mail, your query letter does double duty as a cover letter because it also introduces enclosures like your media kit, possibly a sell sheet, and a copy of your book.

You might be surprised at how many reviewers and other gatekeepers wear more than one hat. Without information about what you expect or want, they won't know what to do with your letter and it may get deleted or deep-sixed. Of course you want to ask diplomatically, but the query must have this request to do its job well.

A great query letter presentation convinces the reviewer that your book is *the* book they want to read. Professionalism is the key. Here are the great query letter essentials:

- When you approach gatekeepers with a query letter (including the owners or editors at review journals), mention how you know about them. Even if you say something as trifling as having read about them in a how-to book, it is an indication that you made an effort to learn the review process. You, of course, may mention this book or my name and it isn't necessary for you to get my permission to do that.
- It is a good idea to mention where you would like the reviewer to post her review if she is not someone specifically assigned or connected to a journal. If you know where they have posted reviews (or their reviews have been printed) in the past, it makes being specific about your needs more tactful and less obtrusive. "I hope you can post your review on Amazon.com and BN.com as you did for [specific review mentioned here]."
- Your query letter needs an opener. The information in the first bullet on this list is a straightforward opener. But a query that starts with a quotation from

your book or an amazing fact that illustrates how important your book is or what it can do for its readers might be better.

> **Note:** It sometimes surprises even seasoned marketers to learn that it is not important to put the author's name in the first or even the second paragraph of a query letter. In most cases, the contact will not recognize the name and thus the most important space in the letter is wasted. You can easily wait until later in the query letter to include that piece of information.

- Next comes a bit about the book. That may include a logline (a very short, catchy synopsis). It might tell how the book fits into classic themes or the current news cycle. It should be something that piques your contact's interest and—when possible—you should know what those interests are by the other reviews they have written or the media they write reviews for.

> **Note:** Most agree that the old idea of telling gatekeepers your book is a cross between two famous books is passé. It sounds clichéd and may sound ostentatious as well.

- Your letter should be one page or less and written in first person.
- It should include a short paragraph on your credentials.

- When approaching a celebrity or well-known person in your field, it helps if you mention that you are considering blurbs for the back of your book. That kind of exposure can encourage a contact to comply with your request.
- Close with a simple thank you and an offer to send the reviewer a copy of your book. Indicate if the book is available in paper, an e-book, or both, and ask them to let you know their preference.
- When you e-mail a query, use the word "query" in the subject line. Follow it with a teaser or headline: "Query for Review of Sci-Fi Book Similar to [another book reviewed by that particular reviewer]." You want your contact to know right off that *you* know who *she* is because an unopened e-mail has no value. Trickery will surely backfire.

> **Note:** Whenever possible send your queries one at a time. To make that easier, save your first query letter as a template but tailor each one to the reviewer or review media you are contacting. When you must do mass mailings, make your letter sound as personal as possible even though it is a generic message.

DON'T TICK OFF A REVIEWER

During the query process you want to maintain your status as a professional but you are also working to build a network of professionals for your writing future.

Reviewers may work for someone else or independently, but they are all free to form an opinion and write about it any way they want. That's because the United States (and some other countries) have free presses. Some authors hate the lack of control, but in the long run, it helps us all because it helps the trust-level readers feel for the opinions so expressed.

Getting reviewers—at first—can be tough. So it goes without saying that we don't want to lose any by appearing unprofessional. After all, you may write another book, and another, so we want to keep our reviewers around especially since we've gone to so much trouble to get them. Even reviewers who don't accept your first book for review may accept the second or third. (I know. Amazing, huh?) See the section in Chapter Five of this book on building lists that also include reviewers, and check Appendix Two for examples of query letters.

Here is a list of things your reviewer does *not* want to hear, especially those who consider themselves part of literary or journalism traditions. It behooves you not to cause them too much work. Reviewing may be their livelihood and they don't think holding the hands of a novice part of their job.

- Don't ask "What publication will this be printed in?" Most reviewers let you know anyway. Some will print and post their reviews in many places and compiling this list can become a chore. But worse, the question sounds ungrateful. I mean, will you refuse to send them a book to review if they don't tell you? You have that right, of course, but the reviewers fussiest about this may be the ones reviewing for traditional and highly respected magazines like *The New Yorker*. If you are interested (and you should be) in giving the review some online exposure on your social networks, your log or your newsletter, you might ask them that question *after* they have agreed to review your book and make it palatable by assuring them you want the link so you can give the review a little extra online exposure.

- Don't say "Send me your e-mail (or other address) so I can put you on my list." Your reviewer doesn't want to feel she is part of a cattle call. Further, this sounds presumptuous. Remember what your mother told you about the word "please." And no, the reviewer doesn't want every one of your promotional e-mails. Do put her on your list of reviewers—you reached her once, you can reach her again. But don't bother her with anything other than a thank-you note or an effort to form a relationship with her using your social networking skills.

> **Tip:** Social networking skills are informed by learning what others are interested in or what will help their careers. They are not about selling your book or getting what you need for your career—at least not until you have earned their trust. And not unless you often and enthusiastically help others out, too.

- Don't say "I'm just checking to see if you received my e-mail" unless an inordinate amount of time has passed. In that case, you can probably say this more tactfully. "I didn't hear from you so I thought we might have had a digital mix-up or perhaps you needed more information to make your decision. I know you review books with a tolerance theme and I chose you because I thought my book a match for that interest."
- Don't say "Please send a copy of the review to me or send me the link once it's done." There are free online services like Google Alert that let you know when your name or the title of your book is mentioned online. Because you probably know who the reviewer is and what entity she reviews for, you should be able to find this information on your own. Once you have become aware of anything from a review—a mention, a quote or the full review—it is to your credit (and benefit) to leave appreciative and useful comments wherever that feature is offered.
- The worst thing to say is "I'll need to approve the review before you publish it." Professional reviewers are often so protective of their journalism freedom they consider the period between the time they accept a review and publish inviolable. Reviewers appreciate your contacting them after they have accepted your book for review or after you have sent them your query letter only if something pertinent has happened they need to know about. Your book won the Pulitzer Prize. Or your book is about midwifery and perfect

quintuplets were just delivered by a midwife in Alaska and the story will soon be dominating the news.

- Oh, I take it back. The worst thing you can do is complain that the review didn't give you enough stars (or cups of latté or whatever) or—gasp!—that it actually critiqued your work and mentioned something you could have done better. That is part of what reviewers do. In fact, it has been shown that reviews that aren't all raves tend to attract more attention and sell more books (*your* books!) than reviews that are all gush and mush. But more on that later.

- Authors should not ask professional reviewers or journalists, "Are you interested in an interview, too." Just like literary agents prefer you to pitch one book at a time in your query letter, reviewers, too, will be more easily convinced if you focus on the review. Professionals must make every effort to keep their reviews from being biased. Furthermore, your contact may be on a deadline. If you are certain that the reviewer—possibly a blogger—also does interviews, wait until the review is done and send a query about an interview after the review has been published (and after you have sent her a thank-you note).

- Avoid annoying little ticks that reviewers and other gatekeepers see so often it makes them yawn:
  - Don't resort to business-ese, which almost always produces the driest business letter this side of the Sahara. It helps if your contact has a

sense of your voice. Avoid words that are too formal or longer than three syllables.

- o Avoid adjectives. Your contact—not you— should decide if your story or writing is "amazing."
- o Don't use the term "fictional novel." A novel by definition is fiction.
- o Avoid saying "I think" or "I believe." A query letter is written in first person by *you*. Your contacts expect that opinions expressed are yours, and those words only weaken your position.
- o Avoid exclamation points.
- o Don't say your book is "entitled." That's the wrong word. It is "titled."
- o For more guidance on the kinds of things that annoy folks who receive lots of query letters, refer to my multi award-winning *The Frugal Editor* (bit.ly/FrugalEditor). I interviewed more than 100 literary agents who shared their peeves—peeves you should avoid that go far beyond grammar and typos. I include sample query letters in its Appendix, and you'll find a couple samples in the Appendix of this book, too.
- When you send a query via post, don't send a book unless your contact's guidelines require that you do so. Offer your ARC or book, of course. Let them choose between a PDF file (an e-book) or a paper copy (a manuscript or hardcopy). But sending a book before you get an OK from them is

presumptuous and an expensive (and unwise) way to use your marketing dollars.

Reviewers like to hear things that log you into their memory banks when you say them. That bodes well for your book—and your next book. Here are a few pleasers:

- "Please let me know if there is anything else you need. I have a media kit I can send by post or attachment, high and low res cover images and headshots, and a sell sheet with complete metadata if you wish." (When you send a reviewer a hardcopy of the book or a manuscript, some or all this material should be sent along with it as part of a complete, helpful presentation.)
- It helps when you personalize your query letter with something like, "I saw the review you did of Kathleen Spivack's *Unmentionable Things*, loved it, and hope you will consider reviewing my book because it is similar in several ways." You would then mention a couple of those ways.
- Of course, reviewers love it when you respond promptly when they ask for information (or anything else). You don't want to get yourself on any reviewer's black (or gray) list. Word gets around in the media age.

Have I mentioned this before? If not, beware. I'll probably say it again! Reviewers love it when you send a warm, authentic thank you for a review. If you decide to send a small gift, too, be sure you send it *after* the review is published so it won't smack of bribery and be sure it is a *small* gift. Professionals in journalism are bound by ethical standards and they may even return gifts. That doesn't mean they won't remember it and appreciate it. It just means they are protective of their independence, their reputations, and their jobs.

CONTROL THE QUALITY OF YOUR REVIEWS

It isn't always possible to get exactly what you want from reviews. Free speech is a constitutional privilege in the United States and other places, too. That freedom—gloriously—applies to our own books as well as to reviewers. Still, there are things you can do to encourage quality reviews without violating the liberties we writers treasure.

Taking control of reviews is seldom talked about because ethical reviews must be as fair and honest as possible. You noticed from the section before this that reputable journalists (including professional reviewers) can be a bit touchy about control, as they should be. Reviews have no value if they can't be trusted. It's one reason we all benefit from Amazon's heavy-handed control of anything that smacks of manipulated reviews. (There is more on Amazon's careful management of reviews later in this book.)

This section is not about how to manipulate the system. It's about how to up your chances of getting reviews, how to help a reviewer do her job, and how to get better quality reviews using ethical practices. Here are some of those processes:

- Carefully research the readers, journals, bloggers, and other reviewers you request a review from—especially those you don't know.
- Try to ascertain if the reviewer is prone to slash-and-burn tactics. If you find any of their past reviews that do this—even if what they say seems true to you or you know what they say to be true—it may be best to look elsewhere.
- Has your new contact reviewed other books in your genre or areas of expertise? If not, might they hate your book based on its subject matter? An example might be asking an avid reader of romance to read a highly literary translation of Russian poetry.
- Avoid teeing them off as described earlier in this chapter.

Sometimes authors are disappointed (though grateful) when they ask their friends, relatives, and those who have read their books to review their book and they say little more than "I couldn't put this book down." That's nice, but the unsaid message that goes out to readers is that it was written by your mom or best friend and that they really didn't care or didn't understand the process. Worse, the powers that be at Amazon.com may delete reviews that are too short or disingenuous in a variety of other ways.

Reviewers who fit into this category will probably be grateful if you tactfully give them some guidelines for writing a review. If you know reviewing is something they are new at, here are some things you can outline for them in note after they have accepted your request for a review or by coaching them verbally.

- Suggest your reader write a review between 100 and 450 words. This one bit of information can help them look more professional and they'll be grateful for that. After all, hundreds if not thousands of people will read it.
- Suggest that your prospective reviewer include their expertise or experience in the review, even if it's just something like, "I have been reading sci-fi for decades and I know what I like." Or, for nonfiction they might say, "I am a chiropractor and found lots of new ideas for marketing my business without seeming unprofessional in this book."
- Your reviewer might compare your book to another they like.
- Ask your reviewer to use keywords you've identified for them in their review.
- Ask your reviewer to tell how they benefited from the book or why it mattered to them. This one piece of information may be the part that convinces a prospective reader that yours is a book worth reading.
- Ask your reviewer not to include a spoiler or at least to forewarn the reader that one is coming.
- Using a bit of humor, you can give these guidelines to newbie reviewers. Tell them you copped this from a fourth grade teacher's lesson book (which is where I got some of them—so it won't be a fib!).
  - What did you like most about the book?
  - Did the book's synopsis or cover information accurately describe the book? How did it differ?

- o Was the book worth the money and time it took to read it?
- o Does this book remind you of another book? If so, name the book.
- o And—perhaps most importantly—is there something you wish the author had covered or done differently?

You can do this diplomatically by telling your reviewer that you are enclosing it for their convenience. You might suggest that it may have been a long time since they wrote a review, and that you hope they might be more inclined to say yes to your request if they had a little guidance.

Note: Do not offer or agree to edit your reviewer's review. A certain amount of distance is a matter of ethics. It goes beyond giving general review writing guidance into the realm of doing the work (that is writing the review) yourself. If they ask, tactfully suggest they get a neighbor or friend to do that for them. You might end up with someone else reading (and loving!) your book. Maybe even someone who will recommend it to someone else.

So far, so good. Now let's talk about how to make a great impression on a reviewer when you send the copy of your book to him or her. When reviewers have access to needed information, they are more likely to write more accurate reviews . . . and their reviews may be more to the author's taste.

Chapter Eight

Sending Your Book to Reviewers

"A gift carefully wrapped as origami and decorated with a bow or calligraphy says you care. Reviewers sense that kind of unspoken respect when they receive a helpful review package." ~ CHJ

Getting a book to your reviewer seems pretty straight forward once you have a published book in your hands. But much of this review-getting and turning-reviews-into-blurbs business must happen long before your precious book comes rolling off the press—whatever kind of press you or your publisher uses.

Authors often get confused about the process in that essential time gap before their books are released. Most first-time authors have no clue that big publishers set the release date (the date bookstores are given the greenlight to deliver books into the hands of readers) well *beyond* the time the book is in print. They do this to accommodate an extended premarketing campaign. It isn't dishonest. They aren't fudging. It's the way it's done. When authors self-publish, they might have no inkling that they should do the same thing. Example: Your print date may be 04/01 and your release date 07/01.

Many of those big publishers use print-on-demand (POD) technology to produce review copies well before the first copies of their offset run come off the press. It's exactly the same technology that many in the publishing industry still vilify when it's used by someone outside the traditional publishing sphere (see Chapter Three, "Getting Past Book Bigotry"). It seems POD is an innovation that is too useful for anyone in the publishing industry to ignore.

These specially produced POD books or ARCs (advance reader or review copies) differ from books sold to the public in important ways. They are formatted to influence and support reviewers and the media. Authors—self- or traditionally published—who decide to pursue reviewers and other influencers with their own advance copies can learn from them. These are the major differences:

- Publishers' POD ARCs might have generic covers (because the real thing isn't yet finished).
- When they do have cover artwork finalized, they might print disclaimers and other markers or marketing material of one kind or another on the cover—usually judiciously placed.
- These ARCs have extra frontmatter pages that include the book's metadata and information on the marketing campaign the publisher plans for the

book. Knowing the projected marketing plan helps the inquiring minds of booksellers and librarians judge how successful a book will be and thus how many copies to order (but, trust me, it is still a guessing game as anyone who has ever been a retail buyer knows). Marketing plans may also be part of the submission guidelines of some of the prestigious review journals. When all this information is included, the sell sheets that get included with other hardcopy ARCs aren't necessary. (There is more on sell sheets later in this chapter when I show you how to make ARCs with all of these features for your own review-getting campaign.)

- These ARCs might include extra pages as part of the backmatter too. Perhaps for extended biographies of the author or information on current and related world events both of which can help convince influencers of the book's importance.

In other words, big presses turn a relatively small run of digitally printed books into an all-purpose prerelease sales tool that doubles as a media kit.

If you are a traditionally published author, you might ask why you would want to do it for yourself if your publisher is doing it for you. The thing is, you may not be able to get your hands on those ARCs to use as review copies. Publishing ARCs digitally is an equal-opportunity technique. All authors—and publicists—can benefit from doing it very nearly free (except for your time, the wholesale cost of each book, and shipping costs—costs you would have anyway but . . . mmm, more frugal). You can—

and you should! You'll learn how in the "Making Your Own ARC" section of this chapter.

THE CONFUSING ARC VOCABULARY

If the vocabulary for ARCs and their sisters has become confusing, welcome to the club. You will sometimes hear terms like *books, ARCs, manuscripts, galleys, PODs,* and *digital copies* used interchangeably when the term *ARCs* would do just fine. For purposes of this book (in the interest of speaking the same language) this is a mini dictionary of terms:

- **Books**. We all know what books are, but we think in terms of finished books. Finished books—appropriately stickered as review copies—can certainly be sent to reviewers. When we do that before a book is released, they become book-like creatures known as ARCs with the addition of support material and perhaps a pre-printed label or two.
- **Manuscript** is the word used for a copy of your book as it looks in your word processor (or looked as you lovingly rolled it from your typewriter and stacked it page-by-page into a manuscript box). When you print it out, it is still a manuscript. Sometimes review journals accept your manuscript for review. Later, when the review is done and the publication is about ready to go to press, the publisher of the book (or the author) is expected to send a finished book. That finished book assures review journal editors that the review they publish

for their readers is, in fact, a review of a *bona fide* book available to the public.

- **Galleys** are essentially edited manuscripts that your publisher sends to the printing press to be set as type before being put on an offset press. Sometimes galleys get sent to reviewers as well. When they do, the publisher may make them a bit fancier by putting them into folders or covering them in some way. The terms *galley* and *manuscript* are sometimes used interchangeably.

  Note: The words *galley* or *manuscript* are rarely used these days. We occasionally see these terms used to describe digitally printed review copies.

- **Digital copies** (AKA e-books and POD books) can be made from any manuscript in a word processing format (like Microsoft Word). Whether e-books or POD books (on paper), these books can be sent by you directly from e-book "publishers" like Smashwords or Kindle to your reviewers.

  Note: Sometimes reviewers order these digital copies directly from Amazon, Smashwords, or other online "publishers" using a coupon, gift certificate, or code sent to them by the publisher or author. This method only works well when the reviewer prefers or accepts electronic (digital) copies in lieu of a print copy or when the book is only published as an e-book.

139

- **PDF files** are another kind of digital copy. When you turn your word processor manuscript into a PDF, it can easily be sent to reviewers or others via e-mail. That eliminates the need for an outside e-mail service to enable your e-mail app to send manuscript-sized attachments. But PDF or not, it's best to get permission to send any kind of attachment to your contacts.

  Note: Many prefer PDFs over word processor manuscripts for both ease of sending them by e-mail and to discourage plagiarizing by outside parties. Some reviewers request them because they can be read on a computer screen and they deem them easier to read than a word processor file.

- **ARC** (an acronym for either *advance review copy* or *advance reader copy*) is a term used for any kind of a review copy that your reviewer or media outlet accepts as a review copy before the release date of your book. An ARC may be a digital or PDF copy (see above). When they are print copies, they may be a special POD run (call them a limited edition of sorts) that might not be completely edited or formatted. Or they may be your finished book doctored up to serve as an ARC. This book tells you exactly how to do the publishing of a specially formatted book to be used as an ARC and how to do the "doctoring" to make copies of your book into a viable ARC including the specific information nccded by your contact that should be included no matter what kind of an ARC your reviewer requests.

You probably noticed that some use the term *advance reader copies* and some prefer *advance reviewer copies*. Most use the term ARC—perhaps because no one seems to agree on what the acronym stands for. Some also use the term ARC when the word manuscript or galley would be more accurate. But no matter what an ARC is at heart, self-published authors or authors who are necessarily taking some of the advance review-getting into their own hands can produce their own. They'll do that mostly to get books into the hands of reviewers so they can read them and write reviews in time for the reviews to be published just before or immediately after the release date.

MAKING YOUR OWN ARC

Making your own ARC or galley takes tons of planning, but you can do it. Many top publishers print a run of books to be used exclusively as review copies using print-on-demand technology (POD) because it is convenient, effective, and economical. They distribute these ARCs by mail to their own list of media, reviewers, bookstore book buyers, librarians, and through special services like Amazon.com's Vine review program. Because I am an Amazon Vine reviewer I am in a position to see lots of these specially produced books and therefore can pass along the ARC secrets of these big publishers in this section on making your own. Now authors of any stripe can print ARCs that are just as professional as the ones big publishers produce. Here is the process.

Jump the galley/ARC process by fudging with the release date of your book. Ask your publisher to list the official release date about twenty weeks to six months from the day your book is set to first roll off the press. I know you won't want to wait, but that lead time will do more than allow you to submit your book to top review journals. It will give you time to get a professional publicity campaign going and to coordinate with your publisher and publicist. It will allow you to use your "real" book as an ARC or to produce a special edition ARC.

Delayed release dates are an industry standard. A book's delayed date *is* the release date. It is the one *you* or your publisher *says* it is and the one you use in your media releases and other documents. It isn't a fake date, so you needn't feel guilty.

No matter how an author is published, she can upload her own unedited review copies (ARCs) free with online services like Createspace and Bookbaby by adding some of the features that reviewers expect in their reader copies. (Keep reading to learn more about those features).

When you have carefully proofed your book, order however many you need for your review process and other premarketing needs. Because these ARCs are not for the public, do not click on the Createspace publish button. You can delete the ARC from your Createspace account once you are through with your launch or leave it there—unpublished for the general public—in case you need it. Once your ARCs (actually your book with a disclaimer and marketing information in them) are in your hands, you send them to reviewers who have shown an interest in reading your book.

If you don't have your book covers or some other aspect of your book finished, plain vanilla (generic) covers are just fine for ARCs as long as they are clearly marked "Unedited Review Copy." ARCs with fully developed covers from your first run of books can also be used as ARCs, but stamp or label them with a violation notice or enclose an insert for that purpose when they are going to reviewers who expressly ask that their review copies not be "defaced."

Note: Disclaimers on ARC copies from the big five publishers are often printed right on the cover of the ARC. They are designated as review copies so they cannot easily be repurposed as gifts or resold. It clarifies to reviewers that they aren't ready-for-the-public copies, that they may still have editing and formatting booboos, and that the extra information they contain in frontmatter and backmatter is for their eyes only.

Hint: I like to use services like Createspace and Bookbaby for ARCs, but I also use them to publish promotion or advertising books, time-sensitive books, books that don't have the commercial value of some genres, and books with niche audiences (like this one). The do-it-all-yourself tracks at these services are especially cost efficient because you upload your book free and might pay only two to five dollars per black and white copy (depending on the size of your book) not including shipping. And, of course, you order only what you need, even just one. These companies' profit margins are built into that price structure, so you are not cheating them by not utilizing all of their services like formatting, interior design, etc. (though you certainly may want or need to use those services). Because I once owned a retail chain that shipped merchandise all over the world, I pay attention to shipping costs and theirs—unlike many online businesses—are reasonable.

It is more expensive and you may have to abide by minimum quantity requirements, but you can also self-publish your ARCs using a printer of your choice or a subsidy press (a publisher who charges you for their services). Many authors use Lulu and I know some who have used Fidlar-Doubleday, Inc. There are a multitude of others for printing books including those on the list of printers (bit.ly/CarolynsPrinterList) I provide on my Web site in the writers' resource section.

You can see that you must decide if you are going to buy finished books or prepublished ARCs from your publisher (if they publish ARCs) or produce your own ARCs. When making this decision, keep copyright laws in mind. The contract you signed with your publisher may forbid you to use your own work (the full book or excerpts) for promotion purposes. Sighhh . . . I hope it doesn't! Such untoward use of copyright law wouldn't benefit you or them.

It's obviously much easier if your publisher provides ARCs to you at a favorable price. You will both benefit. They get the sales that your review-getting efforts produce and you save time and money. You may be able to negotiate publisher support for this process in the contract phase of your publishing journey.

Your review copies also need your book's essential information called metadata. It can be printed on good quality paper and tucked inside the front cover, on a label you adhere to the inside of the front cover, or be part of a sell sheet folded and placed inside the cover. It can also be part of the ARC you publish on your own, meaning that this information occupies the first pages inside the front cover. Metadata includes:

- Official release date—the one you and your publisher have decided on.
- Title.
- Author.
- Illustrator when applicable.
- ISBN, both 10 digit and 13.
- ASIN, when applicable.
- Number of pages.
- Retail price (the price a customer in a bookstore pays for your book).
- Trim size (the size of the finished, final copy of your book).
- Define as hardcover, mass market paperback, trade paperback, or other specification.
- Number of illustrations and/or photographs.
- Publisher's name and contact information—that could be you, the name of your own publishing company if you are self-publishing your book, or the name of the publisher you've contracted with.

- Any other information about your book. Things like diagrams, genealogy charts, etc.
- Distributor's name and contact information.
- Agent's name and contact information.
- Publicist's name and contact information.
- Depending on who you plan to send the ARC to, include the discount you offer to retail stores, libraries, or for educational purposes.

> **Tip:** Check submission guidelines for each journal you query. *Midwest Book Review* asks for books that have not been marked in any way. For them and for reviews you get as your book ages (more on forever-after-reviews later in this book), essential information on a separate sell sheet can be folded inside the front cover. You can also send a review copy to *Midwest* when your book becomes available to the general public because they do not specify that twelve-to-sixteen week deadline.

Here are some other marketing needs your ARC may be used for:

- Beta testing or peer reviews. Authors send a few books out to readers who agree to check them for accuracy or to critique them from a nonprofessional point of view.
- For editors (and others) to use as proofs, to critique, or to review interior design and book cover art and design.

- To give to those instrumental in the success of the book as thank yous. They are often treasured as signed limited editions.
- To give to those who can help expose your book to others. A hand-delivered ARC to the acquisition librarian at your local library comes to mind. So does the feature editor at your local newspaper. Be sure to tuck a query or cover letter into the books you give to media people or other influencers—and a bookmark or your business card.

SENDING ARCS

Sending your ARCs to reviewers (or to gatekeepers for any other kind of marketing) is a little like sending your first child off to kindergarten. She's going to be making a first impression and you want to help her along. To extend that simile, some parents are so anxiety ridden they overdo it. Clean stockings and panties and a nourishing lunch may serve her better than fussing over buttons and bows.

Before you send your ARC to a reviewer or use it for any other premarketing:

- Re-edit and update your media release and query and cover letters.
- Spruce up your media kit so you can send it along with the book copies you send by mail. Remove material in the kit that a reviewer doesn't need.
- Make the review as easy as possible for your reviewer. Be sure your media kit includes a well written sample review. It may help your reviewer

get required facts straight and may even serve as a template for her. If you are unfamiliar with what a media kit entails, check the Index in *The Frugal Book Promoter* (bit.ly/FrugalBookPromo) for "media kits" and read everything on how to produce a professional kit and how to make it serve several purposes for your marketing campaign.

- No gift is necessary and confetti is forbidden.

Sending hardcopy ARCs seems old-fashioned in this digital age, and you may think of a lot of other adjectives for the process, too. Just know you will find yourself doing it a whole lot more frequently than you can imagine if you are just getting started with the review process.

When you send hardcopy ARCs by ground or air:

- Use computer-generated labels instead of handwriting the envelope's address. This seems like unnecessary work, but you are emulating the process that big publishers use. Remember the chapter on book bigotry! When you use computer-generated labels, you are avoiding unnecessarily reminding those in the industry that your book isn't coming from a well established marketing department.
- Use priority mail to send your hardcopy package including your book and support material. It looks great, isn't much more expensive than first class, and USPS and some other shipping services supply the envelope at no extra cost.

Tip: It is courteous to notify your reviewer by e-mail that the copy of your book is on its way. Reviewers are busy folks and it's your job to make their job as easy as possible.

- When a reviewer asks for a copy of your book, write "Requested Material" on the envelope. Please don't pretend it's been requested if it hasn't. You won't fool anyone.

Sending your hardcopy book directly from your publisher, printer, or online bookstore is sometimes called drop shipping. When you drop ship, you only have one shipping bill rather than doubling up on shipping costs from its printing source to your garage or distributor and then again to the reviewer. It is convenient, but you give up the ability to send sales and support materials with your review copy and we know the values of those!

It may not be as expensive as you think to supply one of your own books directly from Amazon to a reviewer. Your publisher still pays you royalties on that book and there is no sales tax when you send your book to some states that don't tax online businesses. You pay more per book, of course, but you also get the benefit of nudging your Amazon sales rank a bit and some of the other benefits of Amazon's lending program when you do it this way.

I joined Amazon's Prime for about $100 a year to get free shipping on most items I order (among other benefits). That doesn't sound frugal but if you buy other things on Amazon often and factor in the savings mentioned in the last paragraph, membership can make sense. It makes double sense if you take my advice to query for reviews long after your book launch. I believe in keeping books alive as long as possible now the Net makes that possible because lower prices on previous books garner readers who may then want to read your new ones (the extra income stream doesn't hurt either). The drawback to using Amazon Prime is that you can't send enclosures, but Amazon does have a little notecard feature that allows you limited communication with your prospective reviewer.

> **Hint:** On the rare occasions I choose to use Amazon Prime shipping for reviews (maybe my stock of books is low just before a writers' conference I'm speaking at), I use one of the windows the online bookstore makes available for the address to type in "Requested Copy."

Many authors choose to ship books in quantity to their offices because it costs less per book to ship many books at once and because they don't want to lose the advantages that support materials mean for influencing the focus and accuracy of their reviews. To dropship or not to dropship? Each author must decide for herself.

Keep in mind that ARCs can be either hardcopies or e-copies as described earlier in this chapter. Either way, the ARCs you send to gatekeepers must have the essentials printed in the book or on the cover or be enclosed as part of the package.

Don't let your review copies go naked. No matter what kind of an ARC you send, a personalized cover letter is a must. Without one your book is poorly dressed.

If you are sending specially formatted and published ARCs you produced yourself, most of your sales and support material will be part of that book. A great cover letter on good stationery should still be part of the package. You wouldn't send a birthday gift to Aunt Martha without enclosing a card, now would you!

Here are other ways to dress up your review package:

- Have labels you need—for mailing, metadata, disclaimers, etc.—printed inexpensively.
- Most authors think of bookmarks as enclosures rather than business cards. They are more expensive, but they're nice to have for some promotions like book fairs and book signings.
- Include an assortment of business cards or bookmarks for your other related books and a couple extras for the book being reviewed in case the reviewer would like to pass them along to fellow readers. If your branding requires it, consider having business cards engraved.

    Warning: Do not do something fancy like include glitter for your fantasy novel. Your reviewer will not appreciate vacuuming up after you. It's also best to avoid tucking in souvenirs that may be practically useless at best or smack of bribery at worst.

If you are letting your finished book do double duty as an ARC, you have more work ahead of you. Here are the essentials for making your book do double duty as an ARC:

- Yep, you'll still need that great cover letter!
- If you are sending copies or galleys that aren't fully edited yet, have return-address size labels printed that say something like "This is an unedited copy for review purposes only." Adhere them to the title page or the front cover of your book.
- Insert a sell sheet inside the cover. It might include a blurb, synopsis, bio, but aside from this kind of information, include the benefits your book provides to the reader. If you send me a request at HoJoNews@aol.com, I will send you a sample sell sheet. Don't feel as if you must follow it slavishly; there is a great deal of leeway for sell sheet presentations beyond using good quality slick and full color so the book cover will look its party-best.
- It's also a good idea to print large labels complete with all the metadata we discussed earlier in this chapter. Apply the label to the inside of the front cover. It is sure not to get separated from your book as sell sheets sometimes do.

> **Tip:** See the section earlier in this chapter under "Making Your Own ARC or Galley" for a list of metadata.

Let me introduce Darcy Pattison. She is the author-publisher of Mims House (mimshouse.com/). She uses the catalogs she produces to dress up her review-getting packages. She says, "The spring and fall catalogs I send out under the Mim's House brand have helped me acquire reviews. Big publishers' catalogs are inspiration for the catalog that I include with the submissions I send to review journals along with my book copy and current press releases." She also prepares a one-page, double-sided sheet with a list of her earlier book covers and recent reviews from major journals. She believes that "when journal editors see that *Publishers Weekly* and *Booklist* have reviewed my books, then I'm legit and they should give the current book serious attention."

Authors who have written other books and had some luck with reviews could follow her model or mention their past reviews in their query letters to obtain a similar result. As an aside, Pattison's efforts are so successful her titles were recently picked up by Overdrive, the company that provides e-books to 90% of libraries in the United States. She says, "The press release announcing our selection of that company went in with every package I sent this month." You may see her spring catalog at mimshouse/catalog.

> **Tip:** You can add incrementally to what a small, flexible publisher might do with the budget he or she allows for the review-getting process. Offer your publisher or distributor appropriate materials to enclose with their prepublish shipments, but don't take offense if they decline your offer.

Sending e-book ARCs by e-mail may—or may not—be the best choice for distributing review copies to reviewers.

Sometimes reviewers *prefer* an e-copy for their review. We love it when they do. We want to keep them happy and we love saving money. Some authors prefer to send ARCs as e-books. It is easier and less costly.

But there are downsides to sending ARCs by e-mail, too. When we use send Arcs by e-mail, we must do everything we can to make up for the loss of some of our influential tools. I think I mentioned before that we want our reviewer to have the format he or she prefers.

Sometimes e-books are the only review-copy choice. The author may have chosen to publish digitally first (or exclusively). When it turns out that e-mail is the best (or only) choice, use these suggestions:

- Yes, you must still have a great cover letter. In fact, it must be super great because much of what your reviewer needs to know will be in that letter. Paste it into the body of your e-mail. No fudging because it is e-mail!
- Your subject line must be professional. Your recipient needs to know exactly what they will find when they open the e-mail. If they don't, they may not open it at all.
- When you send your query letter (your initial contact with the reviewer), put "Query" in the subject line and then a headline-like chosen to appeal to that particular reviewer.
- Once the reviewer accepts your book for review and you have permission to send an attachment, put

"Requested Review Copy" and the book's title in
the subject line.

- Rearrange your media kit to include all the sections
  that might be helpful to a reviewer and none of the
  sections meant for other gatekeepers. Put your
  media kit and e-copy into a zip file to avoid having
  your e-mail rejected by a server.
- Alternatively, regain your marketing edge by
  making a digital ARC using similar techniques to
  the hardcopy ARCs that big publishers produce.
  The how-tos for that are described earlier in this
  chapter.

Gang Chen, author of a series of how-to books for taking
the Architecture Registration Exam and books for taking
the Leadership in Energy and Environmental Design
(LEED) exams (greenexameducation.com/), uses two
alternative e-book distribution methods.

#1. He offers reviewers a free custom-made PDF e-book on
his social networks. He limits the time it will be available
to avoid difficulties later. He alters each PDF he sends by
installing the reviewer's name in the book's header. That
discourages recipients from passing the copy around to
friends for free.

#2. Sometimes he asks prospective reviewers to click on a
link to his Web site where they find another link to the PDF
review copy. He says, "By doing so, I increase the traffic to
my site and end up selling more [of my other] books from
my site, sometimes 50% more."

Tip: Authors who do not have a hardcopy available to send a reviewer must be clear about it in their query letters because many reviewers do not accept e-book copies for review.

Letting reviewers obtain their own copies sounds impolite, crass, and ungrateful. I heard of it only recently when Darcia Helle who has reviewed several of my books of poetry *offered* to order an e-copy of my *Imperfect Echoes* (bit.ly/ImperfectEchoes) using her Amazon Prime membership that allows her one free e-book a month. It was a triple gift for me: A review, a nudge to *Imperfect Echoes'* sales rank on Amazon, and an occasion to learn about another kink in the way the Internet is changing the publishing industry one bit at a time.

There are several benefits when you let a reviewer help out that way. By exploring, I figured out some ways to let online bookstores help distribute your review copies, methods and that opened up new ways to query for reviews, too.

We have always been able to send a review copy as a protected word document or a protected PDF from our own computers when a reviewer requests an e-copy and needs it fast. But reviewers (and others) who are members of Amazon's Prime can download your e-books with Prime or Amazon's lending program at no cost to them or to you.

That can only happen only if you, the author of your book, have agreed to participate in this program offered by Kindle Select, the marketing program Amazon offers books that sign exclusively with them for ninety days. It lets readers who have paid for Prime membership access e-books at no extra cost. You might hear it called Kindle's Lending Program.

I have used this means of getting review copies to reviewers only a couple times since Darcia used it because it seems a touchy thing to bring up unless you know your reviewer *and* you know that they are Prime members. But I also discovered a way to tweet for reviewers who you may not know well but are your Twitter followers (and via retweets, some who aren't your followers!). Here's an example of how you might word such a tweet:

"Calling readers who are part of Amazon's Prime program to review #TheFrugalEditor free!"

You have nothing to lose. Even if the reviews from your twitter requests don't materialize, anyone who goes to get a copy of the free book boosts your sales rankings—and if they retweet, they will help spread the news about your title!

Very few who offer to review from this kind of "query" want a hardcopy. But for those who go that extra step to request one, you could send them an ARC or dropship a paper copy from Amazon directly to the reviewer. That helps your Amazon sales ratings, too! See Chapter Eleven under "Nudge Amazon's Sales Rankings" for more on what great ratings can do for your book and how to manage them.

Authors—especially new authors—are not often convinced that lending books this way (or through libraries, for that matter!) is a good idea. They fear that it cuts into sales. But libraries have been lending books for years, both the books they buy for their shelves and e-books. Lending programs of any kind are good for your book because:

- An e-book that does well may get noticed by Amazon's algorithms. When it does, it may get nudged into system-wide sales promotions.
- Activity on book lending boosts your Amazon ratings every time someone borrows your book just as purchases do.
- Amazon provides a stipend from their KDP Select Global Fund when customers read their books from the Kindle Unlimited and Kindle Owners' Lending Library so the author does get paid.
- Lending allows people who can't afford books (or won't spend the money for them) to read them. Most authors want their books read.
- Readership—purchased or borrowed—increases the buzz about a book that results in more sales. And that goes back to the last bullet point: People who can't afford a book can help create buzz, too.
- It's frugal use of time for authors to use this lending feature to encourage reviews.

Even if you don't choose to ask or suggest this e-book access to your reviewer as a possibility, you should be sure your book is available free (or at a special low price) to Amazon's Prime members. There is no cost to Kindle publishers and authors. It is appreciated by many online readers who may become regular readers of your work. You get a stipend from the Kindle Unlimited Fund when you "sell" a book this way regardless of how it is connected to your review campaign.

The disadvantage of using Amazon's Kindle program (and any other e-book dissemination of review copies) is that it deprives you of a chance to send your media kit, your cover letter, your bookmark, and other aids like your sell sheet that help your reviewer shape their reviews.

Speaking of Amazon, you need to know how these folks can help you early on in your review-getting process. Just turn the page.

.

Chapter Nine
Amazon Can Help Early On, Too

"Amazon may not be an author's cuddliest partner, but we have to credit it for risking much and defying many to bring more books to the masses than was ever possible before." ~ CHJ

I cringe when Amazon booboos. But I hate it even more when I hear authors—often new authors—decide to ignore Amazon in protest against the mistakes the old girl has made since she made her online debut. Amazon has grown to be a powerhouse that recovers from its *faux pas*, but an author who boycotts Amazon based on its past blunders may be putting her entire writing career at risk.

The quotation at the beginning of this chapter explains—at least in part—why I defend Amazon. No one does great things without risk. Along the dangerous path Amazon has taken, they do seem to learn and they definitely are more supportive of authors than they once were.

I could write a book about that the mistakes many chain bookstores—and even some independent bookstores—made that contributed to their own demise. Here's the thing: Authors can survive without Amazon but those who don't try will never know the heights they may have reached if they worked within the system to help Amazon improve and to assure their own success. So, dear reader, don't skip this chapter (or any other in this book) where I tell you how to let Amazon make up for its past mistakes by helping you succeed.

AMAZON'S AUTHOR PROFILE PAGE

The profile page that Amazon offers you free of charge should be installed as soon as you are able to do so—that is from the moment your book becomes available on Amazon. Amazon is always changing, always testing, always improving. It may be impossible to install a page until your first book appears on Amazon, but you should keep checking so it happens as early as possible.

Amazon Profile Page is much like the ones on any social network. You install it through what Amazon calls Author Central or Author Connect. What, you may ask, does a profile page have to do with reviews?

Here's what. Most everything you do on Amazon form links to this page. When your author name appears anywhere on Amazon. Yes! On your book's buy page where reviews appear and on the buy pages of other authors' buy pages when you write reviews for *their* books. In other words, your expertise and experience as an author can be found on your Amazon Profile Page by readers who can access all your books' buy pages, media folk looking to give you free exposure—and yes, reviewers who might be interested in reviewing your book. As your career grows, so grows your Amazon Profile Page.

When your profile page has been properly tended, it also includes other things you do on the Web, like a stream from your blog (which I hope you are also using to extend the exposure of your precious reviews).

Use the magic of Real Simple Syndication (RSS) to install your blog on your Amazon Author Profile Page. You can also install your Twitter feed if it's focused on your writing (and you should have an account that is!). Visitors to your Amazon Profile Page are people who care about you; don't disappoint them.

> **Hint:** RSS is a way that anyone (yes, *you!*) can distribute what you do once—say, on your Web site—to make it appear magically on your blog, too. Or on your social networks. You simply copy and paste computer code. It is a time-saver and effort-expander like none other I can think of.

If you are lucky, your publisher may install this page for you, but they probably won't make it as inclusive as it can be—they may not even have all the information (and links) to make it look cared for. It can be much more than your bio and a list of your books. As an example, you can install the *anthologies* your work has appeared in on that page if you wish. It's a nice, inclusive thing to do. It increases your branding and boosts your credibility.

> **Tip:** I assigned a shortened URL (Web address) I got from bitly.com to my Amazon Profile Page. It is one more place on the Web where readers can follow me and another place besides my own Web site where readers can see all my books at-a-glance and click through to their buy pages immediately. An old adage—as old as anything on the Net can be measured—says something like, "Don't make your contact click any more frequently than absolutely necessary." Find my Amazon Profile page at bit.ly/CarolynsAmznProfile.

AMAZON'S VINE REVIEW PROGRAM

Amazon's Vine Review program definitely is not on my frugal list, but it *will* help you get reviews and it may save you tons of time if you have the budget for it. If you don't, you can use the many alternatives for getting reviews mentioned in this book, but you should still know about the powerful Vine. Actually, there is nothing in the realm of publishing that you shouldn't know. Knowledge is power. So here goes.

The Vine Review Program offers books that pass their muster free to their huge cadre of their Amazon Vine Reviewers. It is used by all kinds of businesses and all kinds of products including books. Though costly, authors and publishers can get many reviews, build a buzz quickly, and raise Amazon's sales rank (or rating) for books.

Generally reviewers talk to others and influence those who read books and buy products. This is true of Amazon's cadre of Vine reviewers, too.

If you are going to spend this kind of money to get reviews (which I don't advise unless you have allotted a budget and are okay with the idea that these expenditures can win big or be lost as surely as the money you spend on a lottery), talk to the Amazon representative about the average number of titles offered in your genre, the number of reviews you can expect to get, current figures on how those reviews might move your book up on Amazon's bestseller lists, and the benefits of that status. Of course, even reasoned estimates are anything but foolproof.

Note: Increasing your number of reviews helps qualify you for other services like AwesomeGang.com. Many require a certain number of five-star reviews before they take you as a client. Some of these services are free. Some—like Bookbub can be very fussy about the books they accept.

Here is what you should know about the Vine program:

- The Amazon Vine program invites reviewers to post their opinions on products. Once they accept you as a client, books that you have sent to Amazon get sent to their reviewers free. These reviews are designed to help shoppers make purchase decisions. According to Amazon, all Vine reviews are independent opinions of the Vine Voices (official reviewers) selected by Amazon.

- Amazon Vine reviews tend to be professional because they must follow Amazon's guidelines. They are honest, fair, and reasonably well written because the reviewers for this program were chosen by Amazon based on feedback from customers and other determiners.
- There is no guarantee you will receive a positive review. Writing a negative review has no bearing on a reviewer's ranking. Thus they are fair, though the reviewers may not be highly educated literary experts.
- You will not be allowed to manipulate your sales rankings by offering an inordinate number of books for review.
- You will not be allowed to approve, influence, modify, or edit reviews you get through the Vine Program.
- Amazon Vine offers different packages for authors and publishers to choose from. Some appeal to publishers with many books and others are fit for your single release.
- You may not contact reviewers personally. (You can leave a public thank you on the comment feature, however.)

  Note: It is generally agreed that vendors (authors) keep public replies respectful, sympathetic, and as helpful as possible. A defensive attitude can only make you look unprofessional.

- Reviewers are expected to claim the assigned wholesale value of books they receive on their income taxes. Most books are assigned a 99 cent tax value.
- A reviewer's rank is determined by the overall helpfulness of all their reviews factoring in the number of reviews they have written.
- Your book will be offered to reviewers alongside books by famous authors published by big name presses, books in all genres, and indie authors, too.

Here is how you make the Vine review process work:

- Enroll your book with Amazon's Vine program.
- Ship the agreed upon quantity of books for review to Amazon.
- Your book will be featured in a queue of books and other products that reviewers can select from.
- Each reviewer who accepts your book for review must submit a review in much the same fashion you use when you post a review for a book you love. That review appears on the book's review stream, but the byline indicates the reviewer is a Vine Reviewer.
- Each Vine review is marked with a link and designation that the reviewer is part of the Vine corps, his or her rating as a reviewer (based on how helpful her reviews are and how many she has written), and—at this point in time—a disclaimer that the reviewer has received a free book in exchange for the review.

> **Note:** Amazon may not like it, but they cannot (and would not) violate constitutional free speech rights by trying to keep you from sending queries to Vine reviewers individually, nor are Vine reviewers discouraged from posting reviews on their own.

AMAZON'S PREORDER PROGRAM

Kindle offers a preorder program to all publishers and authors who are uploading new e-books to their bookstore. It is a benefit that should not be ignored. The big New York publishers have used preorders as a way to promote both their paper books and their e-books to create a buzz for some time. Harper Lee's last book and the last in the series of J. K. Rowling's Harry Potter books come to mind.

Because Amazon still does not offer a program like this for indie-published paper books, it is important that self-published authors plan the releases of their e-books so preorders can benefit both books. Authors who publish only e-books won't have that problem. But all authors should be aware of the loss of exposure if they don't think of some way to use it to their advantage.

> **Note:** I'm thinking that this program will be a boon to authors who published in paper first and still have not published their books electronically. The e-book release cries out for a whole new after-campaign that utilizes preorders for exposure of both iterations of the book.

Amazon's preorder program is a perquisite that cries for at least a few reviews to be installed on your Kindle buy page before your book's release date. As we discussed previously, having great buy pages on Amazon is essential for your Amazon pages to look established.

So, yes. This means you need to get as many advance reviews as you can. That means even if you are published by one of those power publishing houses, you can and should give their review-getting efforts a boost. From what I've seen, you may need to *suggest* your publisher use it and *help* them use it more efficiently. If you are self- or partner-publishing you will probably be on your own with this program from the get-go.

To participate in Amazon's Preorder Program, get current on their guidelines by searching "Amazon's Preorder Promotion." Google "pre-order" (the dash is Amazon's style choice!) to get the most up-to-date information on it.

Caution: When you set your release date, give yourself plenty of time to plan this promotion and get reviews. You need from twelve to sixteen weeks to get reviews from most of the prestigious review journals, anyway. Dr. Bob Rich planned a 100-review blitz for his *Hit and Run* by starting early and letting his reviewers know when his buy page was ready for them to be posted.

Here's what early planning can do for your marketing campaign and review-gleaning process:

- The days Amazon allows you for presales of your e-book helps you build momentum for the launch date—for both the e-book and the paperback.
- Readers will see your promotion and come to your online page to read reviews for up to ninety days before release, though you can do it for a shorter time if you prefer.
- When readers order they may tell others. You could tweet a request that they share their purchase with their social networks.
- I can't stress enough that prepromotion gives your review campaign more impetus, more importance, and that preorders have been highly effective in the past.
- As presales mount, your enthusiasm for marketing and belief in your own success soars.
- Amazon creates your page for you within twenty-four hours. Of course you must give them the data necessary to do it well.
- Preorder sales contribute to your Amazon sales rank. (See more on sales ranks in Chapter Eleven under "Nudge Your Sales Rankings.") Sales rank gives readers and industry professionals an idea of how well your book is selling so your book will have this *additional credibility* starting with the release date.

> **Note:** *The Frugal Book Promoter* (bit.ly/FrugalBookPromo) gives you more guidance for prerelease planning and the Writers Resources section of my Web site at

HowToDoItFrugally.com offers lists useful for your entire campaign and career.

Visit your Kindle Digital Print (KDP) account to set up your new book for preorder.

LOOK INSIDE FEATURES, PRAISE PAGES

Online bookstore peek inside features, your Web site, flip-page widgets for your signature, and your blog allow you to let future readers sample your work. They should be set up as soon as your book is available for presales or—if you missed the window for a presale promotion—it should be set up by your book's launch date. But *now*—whenever that *now* may be—is better than not at all.

Amazon's "Look Inside" feature is sometimes disparaged by new authors, presumably by authors who fear "giving away" much of anything. Perhaps they worry about plagiarizing—but think about it. Readers have been peeking at opening sentences and first chapters of books since print books became available to the masses and plagiarizing isn't exclusive to any one kind of access to a book.

Excerpts (also called blurbs, bullets, endorsements and praise)—especially well-written excerpts—sell books anywhere books can be found. A page or two of endorsements (often excerpted from reviews) just inside the front book cover where people browsing bookstores can easily access them can be the most convincing sales tools in your box. The online "Look Inside" feature works the same way, of course.

If your book doesn't have a page of praise, install one and reload your book to its online bookstore. Traditionally published authors should suggest this to their publishers early in the publishing process. You can add Amazon's "Look Inside" logo to your Amazon buy page through your Author feature which can be found by googling "Amazon Author Connect." It's much easier to do for the e-book version of your book than the paper one, but don't let your publisher decline this important feature that utilizes the reviews you (and possibly they) have worked so hard to get.

There are other services that can help your readers sample your book. I love several of Bookbuzzr's (Bookbuzzr.com) features including help for authors such as book cover design, Web site design, and social media marketing at techhelpforauthors.com and my favorite, their page-flipper widget. Use Flipper as an e-mail signature on your blog and a whole raft of other online applications. I use the social networking icons on my profile page at Bookbuzzr to tweet available excerpts of my book to my followers about once a week. Your profile page on their site doubles as a buy page for your book.

Note: Bookbuzzr allows you to share as many pages of your book—or as few—as you wish. I urge you not to be too parsimonious about what you give away, though. How many words or pages you choose to share, of course, depends on the genre and size of your book, but give your readers your best—and enough to make them want to read more!

So what about those praise pages? You are, by now, used to the term Praise Page. You know what great influencers sincere praise is—whether it's from a reader or an influencer in your topic or genre. You probably have a page of endorsements or great blurbs in your media kit. I hope you have a similar page of blurbs on your Web site—or better still, have them installed at pertinent places throughout your site. You put them on your buy page at Amazon using Author Connect. The important thing is that they are kin to letting your future readers get hooked by reading the first chapter of your book in Amazon's Look Inside feature (or in a bookstore). Praise on the first page of your book and longer peeks at first chapters and other excerpts are your sales force. They're your convincers. They're your closers. Use them liberally.

Next up! Even more ideas for making your reviews and excerpts from them sell books for you.

.

Section IV
You Have Your Review. Now What?

"Second only to holding your new book in your hands for the first time is the joy of seeing its first rave review." ~ CHJ

We've talked about how reviews can benefit both the sales of your book and your writing career. But *you* are the instrument that makes reviews the marketing tool that keeps giving.

Now you have your first review. It is not time to relax. Take a moment to celebrate. Then put your marketing lab coat on and decide what you are going to do with that review. This is a process you will repeat over and over again as you become more adept at getting reviews and adapting them to your promotion campaign. You will become a marketing scientist who keeps asking questions. You will evaluate. Make notes of hits and misses. Remix. And start over again.

Chapter Ten

Making Reviews Work for You

"Very simply put, reviews are the gift that keeps giving." –
CHJ

So you have a review now. Maybe it's your first. Maybe it's your umpteenth. You may be able to determine that sales resulted from it. You may not. If not, you may be disappointed. Don't be. The work a review can do for you has just begun. Here are a few ways you can extend its usefulness.

PERMISSION TO REPRINT THE REVIEW

The sooner we ask for permission to reprint any review we get, the better. That gives us the freedom to use it as a need arises. As our file of reviews-with-permission grows, we come to understand that it is an unmatched cache of promotion jewels.

The best way to get permission to reprint from amateur and reader reviewers is to ask them personally. If your review is in a journal, you may not know who the reviewer is, but you can ask the editor or publisher for permission. Tell either contact you would like to reprint. Ask them how they would like to be credited and what link and other contact information they would like you to use. Just these two questions should suggest to your reviewer that they could benefit from giving you that permission.

Keep in mind that copyright law gives you the right to quote excerpts from a review without asking. So if all your grant-permission-rights efforts fail, you can choose, quote, and credit a positive sentence or phrase from the review when you can't get permission—and when you can—as long as you credit the reviewer. The guidelines for quoting from a review are called *fair use* and they are different from genre to genre and situation to situation. But for novels and full books of nonfiction, Amazon uses twenty-five words as a guideline and I trust they have great copyright attorneys advising them.

> **Caveat:** Getting unnecessary permission can be cumbersome and counterproductive. When you're working with reviews, asking permission can slow you down, but it can also earn you friends as you work with those who reviewed your book. They are influencers in communities of readers. So balance your decision

making process each time you get a review. Think, "Which approach is best for my book and my career?"

So, how do you use reviews once you have them? That's coming, but first let's talk about how you extract valuable excerpts from them.

EXCERPTING FROM REVIEWS

Most of us weren't taught this excerpting business in school, probably because excerpting seems such a nonissue. Many have no idea how to do it *and* don't realize they need to figure it out. They can go miserably astray.

Blurbs may be neglected because there is confusion about what they are. I have heard them called *endorsements, testimonials, praise, quotes, blurbs*, and even *bullets* because they are frequently printed on the back cover of books set off by little BB-sized dots.

When my husband solicited blurbs from VIPs in the Asian community for his first book *What Foreigners Need to Know about America from A to Z* (bit.ly/AmericaAtoZ), he came up with a few other . . . ahem! . . . choice words for getting them. He had been told it is a difficult process. Difficult, but not impossible. He ended up with endorsements from the ambassador to China from the U.S. and the ambassador from China to the U.S. This illustrates why authors shouldn't listen to naysayers who think approaching influencers is futile. You *can* do it and you can do it effectively. Just keep reading.

For purposes of this book, let's just follow the crowd and use practically the whole glossary including *excerpts, blurbs,* and *endorsements.* When we use them, we mean praise or recommendations—even when they aren't excerpted from reviews.

Authors who misuse or underuse excerpts from their reviews are at a disadvantage. Not only are blurbs or endorsements one of the best tools in your marketing kit, but review excerpts are often your only chance to use the credibility of a prestigious review journal as part of your panoply of credit boosters.

The excerpting process is easy and a lot of fun once you know how to do it. Let's say you have before you a review that includes some praise or even a word that made you happy. Perhaps the rest of it wasn't all you'd like it to be. Perhaps (yikes!) it doesn't include your name or title! Here's how to proceed:

- Put on your marketing bonnet and reread your review thinking "soundbites" or the phrases that remind you of the praise you see in ads for movies. Many of them are excerpts or little clips from advance reviews of that film.
- Choose the little gems that make you glad you wrote the book. Some will be very short. Even one word. Shorties are used for everything from restaurants to movies because they emphasize the raves that are . . . mmmm, over the top when publishers and authors use them about their own work. Words like *awesome* and *fantastic.*

- Select some of the praise that points out the benefit a reader might get if he or she reads your book.
- When you must leave something out of the sentence you choose, let ellipses (three little dots . . .) take the place of those missing words.
- Sometimes you need to substitute for purposes of clarity or brevity. If the blurb says, "If there is any justice in the world, this book is destined to be a classic," and you would rather have the title of your book in that excerpt rather than *this book*, you can do that. Remove *this book* and replace those words with the name of the book: "*Two Natures* by Jendi Reiter." You need to put the squarish brackets around the part you insert yourself. So it would read " . . . if there is any justice in the world, [*Two Natures* by Jendi Reiter] is destined to be a classic."

   Note: You can see that your job is to make the excerpt as true to the original meaning as possible without sacrificing its value.

- Stow your excerpts in a file you can refer to later. Be sure to include the accreditation for each blurb. That avoids confusion later and makes using one of them a quick copy-and-paste process.
- Though we should also take care when we quote others, it is legal to quote for certain purposes and in certain amounts without getting permission especially if you write commentary, satire, criticism, academic material, or news reports. Reviews are considered criticism. If you are using your reviews efficiently, you will probably already

have permission to reprint according to guidelines we've already mentioned. (Use this book's Index to look up all the references to copyright in this book.)

- The number of words you can use without permission depends upon the size of the copyrighted work as a whole. Guidelines differ from genre to genre. Find specific guidelines at the Library of Congress Web site (loc.gov/) or let a research librarian help you. The online bookstore division of Amazon protects itself by allowing quotations and blurbs of up to twenty-five words directly from reviews.

> **Note:** Those who want to learn more about copyright law as it applies to authors will find help in *Literary Law Guide for Authors: Copyrights, Trademarks and Contracts in Plain Language* (bit.ly/LitLawGuide) by Tonya Marie Evans and Susan Borden Evans with a foreword by my deceased friend and book marketing guru Dan Poynter.

So you have asked for reprint rights. Or a review journal like *Midwest Book Review* notifies you when your review has been posted and the notification includes permission to reuse it—a very nice service that benefits both *Midwest* and you. In either case, record each permission you are given in a folder reserved for great blurbs and reviews—preferably in a subfolder for each of your book titles. At that point, you are ready to go to work.

USING YOUR REVIEWS AND EXCERPTS

The beauty of reviews and the praise extracted from them is that you can continue to use them as long as you want and some can be used for more than just the book that is being reviewed. An example of that is a review or excerpt from a review that praises your writing style as opposed to the specific title. With that in mind, you are ready to go to work:

- Post full reviews on your blog. The post works best if you introduce it with a little information about the reviewer, the journal, or your personal response to having received it. You can use excerpts in the sidebar of your blog, too.
- To extend the exposure of your review, submit it to my *The New Book Review* blog (thenewbookreview.blogspot.com/). I started it to help authors when I realized it would be a physical impossibility to say yes to review requests from my many readers and students. If you use it, please follow the submission guidelines in the left column of the blog exactly. Because I am frugal with time, I try to make it a copy-and-paste operation.
- Use both full reviews and excerpts on your Web site.
  - o Put your favorite review on your book's page within your Web site. You should have one complete review for every book you publish (and a separate page on your Web site for each book you publish).

- o Use short excerpts from reviews on almost every page of your Web site: In the footer of each page, in a sidebar, and in a table or cell to help break up copy. You may find other places to install an excerpt as your Web site grows.
- o Should you get a review in a prestigious journal, use a phrase like "As seen in *Publisher's Weekly*" on your homepage and other appropriate spots on your site and in your general marketing campaign.
- Announce any new reviews you get on your social networks. When you do this, use a light voice to avoid appearing braggadocio like a Donald-Trump-Running-for-President. He may be able to get away with it, but you probably won't. Instead, frame it as a thank you to the person who gave you the review, the medium where it appeared, or both. Link to the review (that's doing the reviewer a favor) and tag her using the little @ sign so she is aware that you cared enough to promote her Web site or journal. By doing so, you are paving the way to assure she more easily accepts your next book for review.
- Send out media releases (also called—less accurately—press releases) to the local press when you get a review in a prestigious review journal. Use the filter on your contact list to pull out media that might be interested. If you live in a metropolitan area with a major newspaper, they may view this kind of release as clutter, but your local throw-away paper or subsidiary news or feature editor may love it.

- Use an excerpt from your review in any one or all of these places where an endorsement will make people more aware of your book:
  - o Use quotations excerpted from reviews as part of your signature.
  - o Put the *crème de la crème* excerpts from your reviews on the Praise Page in your media kit. For media kits, use short blurbs rather than long ones. Bullets help each excerpt (blurb) stand out and indicates to gatekeepers who read it that you cared enough to make it easy for them. Get step-by-step instructions for writing and assembling a professional media kit in my *The Frugal Book Promoter* (bit.ly/FrugalBookPromo).
  - o Use an excerpt on your preprinted mailing labels as part of your branding.
  - o Use them the same way on your checks.
  - o Feature them on your return-address labels. Your return labels can be much larger than the ones charity organizations send you. I use Vistaprint.com for these. I try to find room for my book cover image and sometimes an excerpt from a review as well.
  - o Use them on the back cover of your book, of course.
  - o In the last chapter we talked about how you can use excerpts on a page of praise just inside the front cover of your book.
  - o Send the excerpt from your review to event planners at bookstores in your hometown or

cities you'll be visiting. Encourage them to post it near the display of your book.

- o Make a short excerpt praising your book part of your query letter for a book signing or workshop.
- o Use praise in the header or footer of your stationery.
- o When appropriate, use or adapt something someone has said about your book as a motto.
- o Use excerpts from your reviews (credited, of course!) in handouts you distribute when you speak or present at conferences or tradeshows. Use them like this:
  - Examples you share in the body of your handout.
  - In the header or footer of your handout.
  - Near your contact information.
- o Use excerpts on your business cards or bookmarks.
- o The U.S. postal service now offers specially printed postage stamps. Did you ever dream your picture might someday land on a postage stamp? Now you can do it (for a fee). Include your book's cover and a brief excerpt from a review. Sometimes you can take a cue from the movie industry and excerpt just one word like this:
  " . . . Scandalous!" ~ *Publishers Weekly*
- o Don't forget to use excerpts (blurbs) as endorsements in your newsletter.

o A thank-you feature in my newsletter (bit.ly/SWWNewsletter) serves several purposes. Yes, gratitude. But it also extends the exposure of my reviews or other promotions. It's about networking. It acts as a resource for my subscribers with links they will find valuable for getting reviews for their own books or to find books for their own reading pleasure. Subscribers who choose to submit their successes also get a little extra publicity.

o Use excerpts from reviews judiciously in the footers, backmatter or frontmatter of other books you publish, or new editions of the book that was originally reviewed.

> **Note:** "Books you publish" might include whitepapers, e-books, or booklets you give away as promotions. Read the case study of my most successful cross-promotional booklets of this e-cookbook in *The Frugal Book Promoter* (bit.ly/FrugalBookPromo). The idea can be adapted to most genres.

o Use one of your pithiest excerpts on the signs you take to book fairs, book signings, conferences, and tradeshows.

Tip: Kinko's/FedEx is a good place to get a poster made and laminated. Floor- and table-standing retractable canvas banners (as seen in photo) are expensive but worth it if you frequently choose these kinds of events because they are sturdy enough to use over and over and easy to roll and fold for travel.

If you decide to pay for advertising think twice. Most authors report advertising—meaning paid-for stuff in the media—is a bust. It generally doesn't result in enough sales to pay for itself. If you insist on taking your chances, use proven blurbs and excerpts from your reviews to give your ads the edge they need. Here are some does and don'ts for that:

- Don't advertise unless you can dedicate a good chunk of your budget to a frequent and focused advertising campaign. If you put your toe in the water and withdraw it too quickly out of disappointment, you are sure to fail. Advertising—done right—takes money *and* commitment.
- Find the perfect media for your ads. That might be social media because their algorithms can focus on the audience best for your book.
- Recognize that it may take some time and trial-and-error to find the perfect demographics of your audience and what these "tests" will cost you during your learning curve.

    Tip: Though an experienced publicist may have media contacts in your demographic, *you* are probably better able to judge your audience than anyone else. Let your publicist work in areas she is more likely to have success with like big-name media she keeps in her frequent contacts list.

- Your blurbs and review excerpts are a proven tool that convinces readers of the benefits of your book. Don't attempt paying for an ad until you have a great one aimed specifically at your book's most likely audience.

> **Tip:** One of your most effective mottoes may be something like "As Seen in *Entertainment Today.*" "As Seen" may refer to an ad or a review in a medium with clout and it is a great alternative if the review doesn't include a knock-out soundbite that can be quoted. This works when you are quoted in major periodicals, too.

Google's AdSense is one of the online programs I tried. I used a freebie coupon I received in the mail and, though personal support Google offered was excellent, I wasn't thrilled with the results for my how-to books which—it is said—advertising works best for.

Some authors report they like Facebook's amazingly targeted ads. But beware: They are not frugal unless they turn out to be a sizzling success. Part of that success may be attributed to Facebook's use of images which Mark Zuckerberg lauded as the most successful result-producing tool ever. I dare take issue with him. Review excerpts (blurbs) are, but the effectiveness of two of them used in conjunction can't be denied. Even then, every part of the ad must be planned perfectly to avoid disappointment. To do that:

- You must choose the perfect demographics (basically keywords) in terms of interests, economic level, education level, and other keywords of your targeted audience.
- You must carefully manage the price-per-click and the limits on your budget for each ad.
- You must have a review excerpt (blurb) that is perfectly attuned to the demographics you are targeting your ad to, and it should be one that is memorable because of the person or media being quoted, because of the impact of the blurb itself, or both.
- Your image must also arrest the interest of your targeted audience. Your most powerful image will probably be your book cover because it is the ultimate brander. It's visual. It gets repeated in many places from bookstores to Amazon even by the most casual marketer.

> **Note:** Great cover design is essential, but it will be more effective if you use a three dimensional image. Gene Cartwright of @AmazonLinks fame offers my readers a special price (https://ifogo.com/3dchj/) to create one.

Using reviews in your media kit is essential. Your kit will be used by all kinds of gatekeepers. Feature editors use reviews as guidelines for their staff writers and sometimes—when given permission—reprint them (credited, of course!). Busy radio hosts may use them instead of requesting a copy of your book to read. Media in general use them to judge the quality of your book and the suitability for their audience. As soon as you have a positive review, add it to your media kit using these guidelines:

- You know this rule: You need permission to reprint a full review.
- Mention that permission has been granted in the header of the review page in your kit where the review lives. Include a request that editors print the review using the reviewer's byline and tagline.
- State where the review originally appeared.
- Key in the reviewer's byline so anyone who uses it doesn't forget.
- When you have many reviews to choose from, select the one written by the most prestigious reviewer or the one that appeared in the most esteemed review journal. Very high praise for your book is good, but reviewer credibility is better. (You may use the very high praise part elsewhere as an excerpt or blurb.)
- If the original review does not include a headline, provide one that is true to the reviewer's intent and highlights what you consider the most important aspect of the review.

If you have a review that isn't as good as you'd like, resist the temptation to edit out the critical part. Media people know a review that is critical of one aspect of your book is more credible than one that praises a book excessively. Editors suspect that a pie-in-the-sky review was probably written by your mother. And, yes. It's also about ethics.

If you have both a short review and a longer one that includes a synopsis of your book, increase your chances of getting some free ink by using them both in your kit. An editor may find one suits her style or space requirements better than the other. Label them "Sample Short Review" and "Sample Longer Review" on their separate pages in the kit.

> **Tip:** If you don't yet have a review, substitute a mini (about fifty to 100 words!) synopsis you wrote yourself until you have the real thing. Use active verbs and third person. Don't give away the ending. It should entice even a jaded reviewer or editor to want to know more about your book. Don't attribute it to anyone. Honesty is especially important in a business that abounds with scams.

> **Hint**: If you want to extract little phrases that rave about your book from a review, they go on your media kit's Praise Page where gleaning the best of the best from reviews and elsewhere is acceptable.

This is a lot to consider after you have mastered the considerable learning curve required to get reviews. It is my hope that the multitude of possibilities for using reviews will encourage you to go after them with a vengeance. After you once have a review, decide how many ways you can repurpose it. Eventually you will build a juggernaut footprint on search engines. That brings you new readers and nurtures your writing career.

SYNCHRONIZING FOR BESTSELLER STATUS

If you dream about taking your book to the top of bestseller lists, know it takes a huge amount of organization and plenty of time. Think in terms of taking all your marketing campaign's promotions and squeezing them into your launch. Use these guidelines to accrue as many sales as possible during your preorder campaign, your launch, or any promotion you use to achieve bestseller status:

- Give yourself time between the printing of your book or review copies to the actual release date (about sixteen weeks) as described elsewhere in this book. Big traditional publishers usually give themselves at least six months lead time.
- Plan launch appearances at brick-and-mortar bookstores that are perfect for your book. Here are things to consider before making your choice:
    - Choose an area covered by a newspaper that publishes bestseller lists. *The New York Times* and the *Los Angeles Times* are examples of the few that do that.
    - Choose a store (or preferably stores) that reports sales to the major metropolitan newspaper in its region that tallies bookstore sales.

Note: To make that selection, choose the store in the area in you can spend the most time doing the most appearances. Consider the amount of support available from friends and contacts in that area (people living there who would likely come to a signing, buy a book, perhaps offer you a room to stay in or host a private launch party for you—though book sales from a private party would not be counted toward the bestseller status you are reaching for).

o Consider the support the bookstores on your short list will give you—support like hanging posters, running a story on you in their newsletter, running ads in the local newspaper, arranging for feature stories in those same newspapers, and featuring your signing in a display window.

Tip: If the store you choose does some but not all of these things, negotiate with them. Or fill those marketing gaps for them along with any other appropriate marketing like radio show appearances on local stations. You should also write and release your media releases in time for all media in the area to list your appearance at that store in their calendar sections or to write and publish feature stories on you.

- Write and release your media releases in time for media in the area to list your appearance at that store in their calendar sections or to write and publish feature stories on you.
- Pitch local radio talk shows and morning and evening drive time radio shows. Fran Silverman (franalive@optonline.net) is an excellent resource for targeted lists of radio programs and hosts.
- Don't neglect online reviews, interviews, and features during the selected period of time for your bestseller putsch. Encourage the inclusion of the names and links of the brick-and-mortar reporting stores you will be appearing at. Have reviews available for reprint to help these online entities meet your deadline before your appearance. (See Chapter Ten for help getting permission from reviewers to allow reprints.)
- If you choose to tackle this effort that can mean immediate stardom for your book, reread the sections on launches, reviews, blog tours, book tours, and media releases in your copy of *The Frugal Book Promoter* (bit.ly/FrugalBookPromo). It will save you money and time and make your overall plan more effective.

> **Note:** If it is too late for you to think about this kind of concentrated campaign, don't despair. There are all sorts of ways to be a bestseller including Amazon.com bestseller status. And *bestseller* isn't the only magic word in a book marketing tool box. *Awards* is another one. *Reviews* is another, and they can be used any

time during the life of your book. Some bestseller lists may not have the traditionally acknowledged prestige of *"New York Times'* Bestseller." but they *can* grow your reader base.

At the risk of sounding like a broken record, keep ethics in mind when working for a bestseller designation. Author David Vise received some very bad publicity for allegedly trying to rig *The New York Times'* bestseller list by buying huge numbers of his own books from reporting bookstores. It doesn't hurt to tweet about bestseller successes, but those in the industry are distrustful and rarely fooled or impressed by most shenanigans authors think up and some have been known to ruin a career.

MAINTAIN RELATIONSHIPS WITH REVIEWERS

When you tend to relationships with your reviewers, you're caring for your future as a professional in the publishing industry. By now that seems like a familiar refrain, reviewers are part of that industry and part of your reading public. People talk. Your reputation is at stake.

Sometimes someone you don't know and haven't queried reviews your book. That makes maintaining a relationship harder. But it is worth the time it takes to track her down to thank her for the gift that made your day. Keep reading for ways to find her.

Attending to your thank-you notes never goes out of fashion. Your mama taught you to do that a long time ago. Reviewers need love, too. When they write a review you love, write a review you don't love so much, or even when they write a review that convinces you to read someone else's book, send them a note of congratulations.

With very few exceptions, you want to keep in touch with your reviewer. Here are some easy and quick things you can do to foster goodwill immediately:

- Send your reviewer a thank-you note. If possible, use a greeting card or real paper. Vistaprint can print your logo on thank-you sized stationery relatively inexpensively and your logo, name, and book cover image make memorable branding.
- Send along a small, thoughtful gift. This must be done *after* the review appears so it cannot be interpreted as a bribe. I sometimes send one of my poetry chapbooks or my little booklet of wordtrippers, *Great Little Last-Minute Editing Tips for Writers* (bit.ly/Last-MinuteEditing). Both retail for about the cost of a greeting card.
- If you promote the reviewer or link to their review (the review's online address), let them know and give them the link to your promotion. They may drop by to leave a comment on your blog or virally extend the reach of that link to their own networks.
- We talked about asking reviewers for permission to print reviews, but you can also request they post their review elsewhere—say, at BN.com or other online sites that allow readers to post a review like the famous Powells.com.
- And the biggest, most important thank-you idea of all: Send a letter to the reviewer's editor praising

her review-writing staff or freelancer. That editor is probably the reviewer's boss. Since your sincere praise can make a difference to the reviewer's writing career, she's sure not to forget you!

Caveat: If a reviewer does not respond to your gestures, do not press her. If she does, it is an indication that she will appreciate at least some modicum of interaction or networking.

Other occasions where notes may be appropriate include sympathy, holidays, birthdays, and as your friendship grows, postcards when you travel. Social networks can help you track those occasions. When you have your reader-reviewer hat on, you do it to give back to the industry and to make a fellow writer happy.

Send congratulatory notes when reviewers and other media friends receive awards, redesign their Web pages, write a great feature story, or are assigned a new column. If you have your preferences set for it, LinkedIn will let you know when these occasions arise among your contacts there.

Notes create goodwill. Goodwill creates opportunity. Use your writing skill to make the recipient feel valued rather than a cursory note like the ones you tried to get away when your mother insisted you thank your librarian auntie who always sent books for your birthday.

What are the rules governing thank-you notes? You didn't really think I was going to give you firm, fast rules, did you? Reviewers, authors, and titles differ and each review poses a unique opportunity. That means you will have some evaluating to do. As you decide how to thank your reviewer, consider that there are two basic kinds of reviews—those written by professional reviewers and those new to the world of writing reader reviews.

Professional reviewers include reviewers who get paid to write reviews. (But not by you! We talked about that in Chapter One.) These are journalists or freelance writers paid by magazines, newspapers, review journals and the like to write reviews. You may know of them, but you'll seldom know any of them personally.

Hint: There is an unwritten rule among many professional reviewers: If they can do no more than slash and burn, they return their review copy with a note much like the ones you get when a submission has been declined. It would look something like, "It seems I am not a good match for your book (or title)."

On the other hand, reader reviewers are not professionals. They may or may not know the niceties or processes expected of professionals and you should keep this in mind when working with them, including your thank-you notes. Examples of reader reviewers are those who drop by to leave comments or full reviews on Amazon or Goodreads (though sometimes they are professional reviewers, too!). I told you the rules are not always distinct.

Another big difference. Reader reviewers are often not the recipient of a manuscript or ARC from either you or your publisher. These reviews may appear out of nowhere.

Your thank-you notes to both of the classes of reviewers may be about the same in most cases in which the reviews have been fair, honest, and include both praise and criticism. Generally the note will be a gracious, warm thank you. You will probably choose to ignore the critique part unless you can honestly acknowledge that you appreciate their input or that you plan to utilize their suggestion in the next edition or your next book.

> **Hint:** Your most memorable note—the one that turns out to be the most instrumental in your writing career—may be the one you send to a reviewer who was critical of your book. One of my least favorite reviews for my first novel was written by Rebecca Brown for her Rebecca's Reads Web site (rebeccasreads.com/). I told her—sincerely—that I learned much from her critique. I kept in touch with her and it wasn't long before she occasionally published my articles or essays on her site.

Getting a thank-you note to a reviewer can sometimes be problematic. There is only one firm rule about sending thank-you notes: A thank-you note sent on real paper with a real postage stamp to a reviewer's place of business or home is always preferable to any other method.

Having said that, we know that is not always possible and an author can only spend so much time finding contact information on the Web. Further, e-mail thank yous are becoming more acceptable in business situations (but that means that real handwritten notes are all the more memorable).

Try finding the reviewer's personal or business Web site. It might include her address or the address of the journal or other media she works for. A note sent to a reviewer in care of, say, *Kirkus* reviews, has a good chance of being forwarded to her.

See what you find by searching on the reviewer's name using Google, Bing, or your favorite search engine. Here are some ideas for following through:

- Search for the reviewer on a few social networks and send her an electronic message.
- To find reviews (and other mentions) you may otherwise never learn about, subscribe to services like Google Alert. When you list your title and your name with them, these services send you a magic notice to your e-mail box with a link to the review. Really!
- If the reviewer is a blogger, leave a comment on her blog. This one acknowledgement will put you ahead of (just guessing from experience here!) 90% of authors. I know authors are busy. I know some authors get lots and lots of reviews. But, still . . . .
- Try clicking on the link that online bookstores usually provide for the reviewer. This might lead to his or her profile page or something similar and there you may find other contact information—usually online contact information.
- On occasion I feel I can ask a reviewer for her address in an e-mail or private message on Facebook. The reviewer may send her street address or a PO Box number. If she declines, that is your

opening to thank her in any number of less formal ways.

- When all else fails, I've been known to tweet. It might work even if you can't identify your reviewer's Twitter name because she may be notified with an alert program that searches on her name. My tweet might go something like this:

  "Sigh! Couldn't trace a wonderful Amazon review for #TheFrugalBookPromoter from Ann Eidson!" You could put a link to the review here, too, depending on space, something like bit.ly/GreatReview.

RESPONDING TO NEGATIVE REVIEWS

Each of us may face a negative review eventually. Reviewers are human. They have different tastes, expectations, and agendas. It might be more comforting to remember that the most successful authors may face them more frequently than the more obscure author.

Warren Adler said, "Every serious novelist worth their salt believes in their soul that they have written a brilliant novel . . . in which the reader will find compelling characters engaged in deeply imagined stories that profoundly illustrate the human condition." I suppose Adler's take on authors' assessments of their own work applies to nonfiction writers, too. I certainly strive to make my HowToDoItFrugally series of books (one series for writers and one for retailers) a cut above others.

Of course writers must believe in themselves and their art to finish the gigantic task of writing a book clear through to those final four hashtags we install on the last page to pat ourselves on the back for our accomplishment. We're still fooling ourselves if we suppose that everyone loves the kind of book we write or our book in particular.

Adler also reminds us, "*Moby Dick* was declared 'dull, dreary, and ridiculous' and Orwell's *1984* 'a failure.'" In the publishing world they say both bad book reviews and effusive praise come with the territory. Just celebrate you are being noticed, and be sure your name is spelled right (the same mantra recited by Hollywood stars).

"Getting your name spelled right" is more important in this day of search engines than ever before. But think twice, count to ten—or maybe 100, and sleep on it before you shoot back any other kind of comment to a reviewer or journal that had the nerve to critique your work or was so miserably unprofessional to spell your name wrong.

Consider whether there is something to learn in the critique—even if the words stung and you lost sleep over it. Consider how you might come off as unprofessional and thin-skinned if you protest. Consider that what you write may get quoted for the public to see.

You might also want to consider if there is any benefit to you. As an example, some would say that when Jonathan Franzen began a dispute with Oprah Winfrey over his famed *The Corrections* (bit.ly/TheCorrections), he produced more in book sales than he lost in reputation when the media grabbed it and had a lark spreading the news everywhere. Of course, Franzen was already a known author and Oprah has an . . . ahem . . . small following of her own. So this little tiff was sure to *be* news! It's likely that you don't already have two big names on your side—at least not yet.

Still, you might benefit by emulating Franzen's chutzpah. To do so you must master the art of turning negative publicity to your advantage or hire a publicist experienced in doing that for you. Your experience must have the necessary elements for a publicist to effectively work with. You must be willing to spend the time necessary to participate in the buzz you or your publicist creates for you. It's also a good idea to factor in whether such publicity will sell enough books to cover the fees a high powered PR person with experience in conflict exposure would charge you or the time it would take away from your precious writing schedule.

My advice is, use your deep breathing skills or pay for a couple sessions with a therapist instead.

Of course, there are certain situations that may require action on your part. Here are a few:

- If the reviewer did spell your name wrong (or forgot to use it) ask her or him to fix it—tactfully. That means including a thank you for the review along with the request. It was just an oopsie, after all.
- If the reviewer spills the beans about your surprise ending and it can be corrected, ask her to do so. If

she can't, don't refer your readers to that review. On the other hand, if a spoiler appears in a super newsworthy journal that should know better, their mistake and the luster of their name might rub off on your book if you let it be known on social media, etc. Much depends on your personality, how much time you have to spend on this kind of publicity as opposed to spending the same amount of time on more positive marketing—like getting more reviews.

> **Tip:** If the journal offers to fix a review *faux pas* with a correction in the next issue, it may only exacerbate the problem. That it might also add to the exposure of your book is an upside. Only you can decide which you would prefer. You might also hold out for a rerun of the review complete with proper edits, but your chances for success with that kind of request are slim, due to time, space, and policy restraints.

- The reviewer gets something wrong. Intentionally, out of ignorance, or by accident. (By that I *don't* mean that she expressed an opinion you don't agree with.) Ask her to correct the error, but also find something she did right and thank her. Your job is not to burn bridges, as they say. You have a career in writing ahead of you.
- When an error occurs on a blog or some other place on a Web site that allows comments, you can often use that feature to correct minor errors. However, it is a courtesy to the blogger, reviewer, or reporter to

let them know so they can correct the error before you take matters into your own hands.

> **Note:** When a reviewer criticizes an aspect of a book (say, she somehow confuses the name of the protagonist with the name of the antagonist), it is important for the author to examine her work to see if anything could be done in terms of technique to avoid that kind of criticism (or misunderstanding) in the future.

A couple of techniques for responding to a criticism that may have merit comes from publicist Sandra Beckwith (buildbookbuzz.com) who wrote an article on responding to negative reviews for Independent Book Publishers Association's (ibpa-online.org) print magazine, *Independent:*

> "You're absolutely right—that rule has changed since the book's publication. I'll make sure it's updated in the revision. I appreciate that you pointed it out so I can improve the text."

or

> "At first I was disappointed to read that you thought the dialogue was a little stiff, but then I started thinking about how I could fix that in my next book. Would you be interested in being a beta reader for it? If you'll send me your e-mail address, I'll send you more information."

Here are a few inappropriate review models and other occasions that might be best ignored:

- The reviewer was not suited to review this book. She admits to hating horror novels, as an example, and reviews your horror novel as if it should be something else.
- The reviewer has obviously not read the entire book. Sometimes she admits as much in the review itself.
- The reviewer obviously has a prior agenda, has written a book that competes with yours (or has an author friend who has written a similar book), is angry, has some axe to grind, or has a world view that differs from yours. If you challenge her, she may welcome an occasion to carry her scheme to another level. Like some politicians, she may double down and do it in public. You probably don't want to risk playing into her hands. Or you don't want to take the joy out of writing and feel ignoring her is the best tactic.

    Hint: Know that if a reviewer exhibits a bias that is obvious to you, it will probably be obvious to your future readers, too.

- When you don't care to do so. You're too upset or angry or have any other reason for not wanting to deal with the problem.
- When the review is on Goodreads.com or similar reading social networks. Administrators discourage

direct contact between authors and reviewers and may bar you from their site.

- When a reviewer claims your book has nothing in it she can't find elsewhere on the Web. All we must do is read Joseph Campbell's wonderful books on literature to know there is no such thing as something entirely new and that all literature—and certainly nonfiction—is built on the bedrock of ideas, research, and theories that have been in circulation before. Further, we all know how much more we can learn from an author who has vetted, researched, and given an author the benefit of her experience than we could from floating willy-nilly around the Web to read piecemeal. I doubt you want to spend the time arguing this point or that you would have much success if you did.

Here's the most important thing about reviews—one that is so important to your success and peace of mind I have mentioned it before: A review that intersperses some critique along with praise is more credible than nonstop raves. This has been proven in studies. Even more important, though, is that the author should not begin the review process with any expectation that it will be otherwise. Nothing is perfect. No author can please every reader.

Studies have also shown that an entire list of five-star reviews for any given book may be suspect. In fact, many readers head straight for the one- or two star reviews for their evaluation process. I have seen many authors get upset (and take personally) a three- or four-star review that they should have been thrilled with.

And here is another little tidbit to reassure you: Charles Dickens' entire career was dismissed by this statement: "We do not believe in the permanence of his reputation." Reviewer arrogance is always possible, but it is far more frequent that reviewers—who are, after all, writers too—prefer to help an author do well and are willing to spend time reading a book and reviewing it to help it get the exposure it deserves.

Your promotion souvenirs might at first seem like a frugal way to thank your reviewers. They seem suitable because they tend to be inexpensive and gifts to the media shouldn't smack of payola.

But here's the thing. I have rarely seen giveaways for media kits or other promotion used effectively except when they are used to attract editors to take media kits from the pressroom at a tradeshow. Even then, something with a higher perceived value than "souvenir" is more likely to encourage editors with press badges to pick up your kit, take it back to the office, and possibly feature you or your book in whatever media they represent. This is one time when a copy of your book with a bookmark and a cover letter with a pitch for a feature story makes the best impression and is also reasonably frugal. People who use the press room tend to be influencers. It takes only one interview or feature story to make that expense seem like a bargain!

I advise my clients to skip souvenirs for the most part and spend their budget on something that will extend goodwill among gatekeepers—radio hosts, feature editors, and yes reviewers. By "extend goodwill" I mean something that hangs around where it will be seen—preferably something with an endorsement printed on it. Otherwise, a handwritten thank you will make an impression and be more than adequate. It, too, will be more effective if it's imprinted with a favorite blurb!

If you do decide to buy gifts as thank yous (and perhaps use them in other ways), they should be suited to the theme of your book.

I viewed my first promotional item more as a thank-you gift than as advertising. I wanted something that suited the material in my book, but I hadn't yet learned that most of the stuff authors were spending their money on was not effective. I bought miniature thimbles with "Utah" printed on them for my book's launch because it is set in that state. My mother made little felt slipcases for them and my husband tied tiny gift tags with a quote from the book to each pouch with thin grosgrain ribbon. Mom refused to make more than the original 1000 pleading poor eyesight. My next promotion gifts were miniature hand-crocheted doilies made in China, presumably by women with better eyesight. We used similar tie-on tags. These worked better than thimbles because they more easily lie flat in books, envelopes, or thank-you cards. But think of the expense. Think of the time. Think of the guilt I felt about those poor Chinese women once I had time to think about it!

Each of these gifts had something to do with the sewing imagery in *This Is the Place* (bit.ly/ThisIsthePlace) and *Harkening* (bit.ly/TrueShortStories). Linda Morelli makes artistic blank journals and notebooks by hand for prizes and contests that would be ideal, useful thank-you gifts, too. Someone might be so impressed they would tweet about it!

By using case studies (or experiencing a situation) we begin to see that this gift-buying process is more about goodwill and name recognition than about their effectiveness in terms of book sales. Once you've altered your perspective, your serenity quotient goes up. Here are guidelines to help make a decision about your thank yous and your souvenirs when you think you absolutely must have them:

- Shun the politically incorrect unless your book is a steaming gossip sheet. Avoid smoking accoutrements unless the title of your book is *Up in Smoke.*
- Hand or homemade items are appropriate only if those qualities are integral to the image you want to project. Unless you are a graphics and computer production whiz, handmade bookmarks—unlike some homemade gifts—might as well be printed with "Don't buy my book. I'm an amateur."
- Most gatekeepers appreciate food, but your edible should tie into the theme of your book unless the food is a thank you after the fact. Publicist D'vorah Lansky (reachmorereaders.com), once sent me brownies as a thank you for participating in one of

her seminars. That was years ago, and I haven't forgotten it.

- Buy in bulk to keep costs down but don't be overly optimistic. Your needs will change.
- Flat is best. Lightweight is a plus. Green, these days, is a plus-plus.
- Consider cost and distribution. You can easily give away thousands of promotional gifts and if you restrict distribution because of the expense, you may defeat your purpose.
- To be truly frugal, settle for printed thank-you notes—perhaps even engraved depending on your branding—with your name, the title of your book and a buy link or your Web site. If the paper and print quality are good and the note is handwritten and sincere, no gift is needed. I mean, people rarely receive a thank you, much less something that comes in the mail and is handwritten.

> **Warning:** No matter how it's used—from a thank-you-for-the-review gift to handouts at book fairs—a promotional gift without contact and how-to-buy information loses its effectiveness. In some cases, it may annoy the recipient who must then expend time and effort to contact you or get the information she needs about you or your book. The lack of a blurb or endorsement somewhere on the item is a missed opportunity.

The hard work is done. As your writing career progresses, you will amass dozens if not hundreds of reviews. But thanks to the digital world and the likes of Amazon.com, you can use them more effectively than ever before. Tricks for doing that are up next. So put on your review-managing beanie and fasten your seat belt.

Chapter Eleven

Managing Your Amazon Reviews

"Don't let anyone fool you into thinking you can relegate book sales to your own Web site sales page and succeed. Readers look for information more often on Amazon than on your publisher's site or your own." — CHJ

To sell your book to someone other than your mom and best friend, you probably need to learn more about the powerhouse bookstore and the search engine Amazon.com has become and how reviews fit into that picture. They will be even more powerful as their brick-and-mortar stores grow from their flagship store in Seattle to the projected four hundred across the US—and perhaps the world—and now that Amazon is an online presence in the UK, Germany, India, Mexico, Japan and more.

The sections in this book on using Amazon and other online bookstores to their fullest potential is the most essential advice in this book and you need reviews to give it the tender, loving care it needs. Really.

No one who knows publishing well ignores Amazon's sales pages—including the big New York publishers—but few (including the big New York publishers) do a good job of utilizing the features it offers, including book reviews. You need to know how to avoid getting yourself into hot water with Amazon as you go about getting reviews and how to manage those reviews once you have them. Knowing how gives self-published authors an edge over the big guys and if you are published with the big guys, you can increase your visibility beyond what their marketers do for you.

To do all of this, you need to see how most everything you do on Amazon affects its search engine and algorithms. They can affect your exposure and that exposure translates into sales.

> **Tip:** With Amazon's power in mind, use the Index in this book to find and explore the many features Amazon offers writers like Author Connect.

Your reviews on Amazon (along with who knows how many other factors) boost the algorithms Amazon uses that can end up anointing your book with all kinds of benefits for both your paperback and Amazon's Kindle division.

NUDGE AMAZON'S SALES RANKINGS

Great sales rankings on Amazon may not be something readers notice, but influencers in the publishing industry sure do. You'll notice, too. As your rank improves, you'll feel better about your online marketing efforts and you'll see your royalties soar.

You need only a few essentials in your Amazon tool box to build the traffic crucial for your reviews to be seen—and to convince readers to buy your book. *This* book helps you get the reviews that influence Amazon's sales ranking and this section gives you everything else you need to maximize them.

Amazon sales rankings are dandy little aids for evaluating how your book is selling. Not that you should fixate on them, but having an indicator that your book might need a little sales boost is nice. And—when those ratings are nurtured—they prod Amazon's algorithms to lead people who read books similar to yours to *your* Amazon buy page.

The problem is that most authors and publishers know little if anything about how those rankings come about. That isn't their fault because I doubt if Jeff Bezos, the brains behind the entire Amazon model, knows exactly what his algorithms measure. If they're anything like the rest of the Amazon site, they change from day to day anyway. You don't need to know the magic behind them; you do need to know what they are and how to prod them a little:

- Find your sales ranking (or rankings) on your book's buy page under "product details." Often called "metadata," these details are the specifics for your book like ISBN, publisher, number of pages, etc. Scroll down a bit to find this section on your page.

- If you have a ranking of 24,800, that means that 24,799 books listed *in your category* are selling better than your book and that up to millions of books in your book's category are selling less well.
- The lower your sales ranking number for your book the better. Sales rankings for your Kindle (e-book) page will not be the same as the one on your paperback page.

  Note: When the pages for your paper book and e-book are digitally connected properly, your reviews will be the same on both pages. (There should be a link on each page pointing to the other.)

- If you market and promote, your efforts may lower those rankings (lower is good!). If so, celebrate because this doesn't always happen. Sometimes the marketing you are doing does not improve your rating at all, though it should contribute to your overall branding effort.
- Don't try to translate a drop in your ratings to the number of books sold. The algorithms are a lot more complicated than that.
- Sales rankings fluctuate (sometimes wildly) during the day.

  Warning: Do not spend a lot of time checking your ratings. They should be used as indicators. They shouldn't become an obsession. It's best not to obsess, but if you can't avoid it, Bookbuzzr.com and others provide services available for pinging ratings to you in your e-mail box.

Influence Amazon's sales rankings by placing your e-book in categories that have the least competition as long as those categories truly reflect the content of your book. At this point in time, you can't influence your paperback categories because they are determined by BISAC categories—the ones that indicate where your book will be placed on library and bookstore shelves. To find the right category for your e-book on Kindle:

- Log onto Amazon.com.
- Click on the dropdown box near the search window.
- Highlight Kindle Store on the dropdown list and leave the search bar blank. You aren't searching for a specific book's page. It's the Kindle *entry* page you're after.
- Hit go. In the left column you'll see Kindle E-books or Books. There you'll find categories with numbers indicating the number of books in each category. Look for the categories that best suit your book *and* have the *lowest* number of books in that category. Keep clicking on the categories until you find the smallest subcategory under each of the larger ones that suits your book.
- Check categories for your book occasionally because the popularity of categories changes and new categories get added from time to time.

Note: Don't fudge categories too much or your readers won't find your book when they search on applicable keywords.

Once you have suitable categories:

- Go to your Amazon Author Connect (also called Author Central) page and click on "contact us" link.
- Send the Amazon tech elves an e-mail requesting two categories you've chosen. Each will be a string of individual categories you have chosen for your book in descending order—the largest category first.
- Or better yet, have Amazon call *you* using their contact feature. Tell the customer service person which categories to delete and which to add. (You theoretically only get two categories, but three often appear so it doesn't hurt to request a third.) Amazon seems to take care of these requests within a couple of days.

Here is an example of how those rankings look. I copied this from the buy page of my *The Frugal Editor* (bit.ly/FrugalEditor) on a random day:

Amazon Best Sellers Rank: #557,109 Paid in Kindle Store (See Top 100 Paid in Kindle Store)

- #87 in Kindle Store > Kindle eBooks > Reference > Writing, Research & Publishing Guides > Editing

- #255 in Books > Reference > Writing, Research & Publishing Guides > Writing > Editing
- #733 in Kindle Store > Kindle eBooks > Reference > Writing, Research & Publishing Guides > Publishing & Books

> **Note #1:** The first entry "labeled #87 in . . ." qualified *The Frugal Editor* (bit.ly/FrugalEditor) for inclusion in Amazon's top 100 books in the Kindle Store *in that category*, not in the top books on the whole Amazon site. When your book is in the top 100 either on the whole of the site or in a category, it *is* a bestseller, but you must make the *category* clear when you promote it.

> **Note #2:** I picked a random day for showing you what the rankings for my *The Frugal Editor* (bit.ly/FrugalEditor) look like. Somehow I got three choices rather than two. Maybe that's because Denise Cassino helped me with rankings, but it may be because Amazon changes everything frequently—from the positions of different features on their pages to their policies! Denise is an Amazon expert. If you are looking for a hired hand to help you with this project, she is one of the best. Reach her at dencassino@gmail.com.

- When your book does well enough to make the algorithms extremely happy, you qualify for several of the benefits Amazon offers to bring your book to the attention of readers who might be interested. That includes their direct-mail campaigns, their bestseller lists, their discounts and other perquisites.

- When you use Amazon's Best Seller Rank to market your book, keep it honest and light. Here's an example of a tweet I use that clearly identifies its bestseller status. Having an example like this serves as a model for presenting your bestseller status honestly:

> "Yay, my #TheFrugalEditor is on Amazon's top 100 editing books bestseller list today! Bit.ly/FrugalEditor"

Here are the most important specifics for you to pay attention to:

- Notice that I'm specific about the category that *The Frugal Editor* (bit.ly/FrugalEditor) is "tops" in. It's not nice to fool Mother Nature—or readers!
- Notice also that I have a registered hashtag. That is one way to let Twitter followers learn more about your book within the 140 character limit. Go to Twubs.com to get one for your own title. I swear by the registering process they offer for additional exposure for whatever you are promoting including your reviews. You may want to use my #GreatBookReviews hashtag for linking your own reviews to the wider world of readers.
- Notice that I use shortened URLs (Web addresses) whenever possible. I like to use bitly.com for that. It is free and allows you to brand your links by

changing out real words for gibberish like
"x54321Y."

- One thing this example doesn't show is that I try to
use the links (social network icons) found on my
book's Amazon page instead of posting directly to
my social networks. That may nudge Amazon's
algorithms toward giving me some of their other
benefits.

> **Note:** Yes, your *reviews* are—according to the
> people most familiar with Amazon's secrets—
> part of what those algorithms look at to push
> your book to even greater stardom.

Find more tips and articles on topics like this in my
SharingwithWriters newsletter and get a free e-book by
subscribing at howtodoitfrugally.com. You'll find a
subscribe window in the top right corner of almost every
page of the Web site.

WHEN AMAZON REVIEWS GET YANKED

Occasionally Amazon yanks a review from your buy page
and they usually do it without notice. When this happens it
is only natural for an author (or reviewer) to be upset. Do
know, though, it is not necessarily an attack by Despicable
Me wearing an Amazon hat. Amazon often has good
reasons for disappearing reviews, most of them designed to
maintain the credibility of the entire review system. They
seem to be motivated by their best instincts. I am reporting
one of their efforts to bring the quality of their reviews up
(keep reading) so you can see both the positives and the

pitfalls. That knowledge will help you better manage your reviews—both the reviews of your books and the ones you write for others' books.

Amazon made the front pages of the business sections of top newspapers by taking legal action to stop fake reviews and reviewers. I call them fake (as many do) because these reviews and reviewers undermine the credibility of the review process and weaken the entire system readers use to identify books they want to read out of the many hundreds of thousands published each year. So when the *LA Times* reported that Amazon sued more than 1,000 writers for selling recommendations (and reviews!) for books (and other items) they didn't buy, I was squarely in Amazon's corner. I don't think any author would argue that improving the credibility of its reviews is a not a noble cause, though it may not be working as well as Amazon had hoped.

Note: For the full *LA Times'* story, see the Technology page in their business section, Thursday, October 2, 2015.

Amazon sees reviews that are too glowing as a danger sign. That's fair. Professional reviews *can* be rave reviews, but no book is perfect. You've heard me say it before: A review is more trustworthy (and therefore sells more books—proved by studies over the years!) if it points out weaknesses as well as strengths. Such critiques needn't be snarky. They can be tactful, firm, and helpful to readers and the author alike. So, perhaps those oh-so-awesome reviews are among the "fake" reviewers Amazon is after.

It was reported that Amazon was also after Fiverr.com. Fiverr's customers offered reviews for $5. You already know how I feel about pay-for reviews, but many of these were worse! Some *promised* five-star reviews. And, yes, this is—to put it mildly—dishonest. Tactics like these could end up being harmful to the author, to the person offering the unethical review, and certainly to the reviewers' readers who are in most instances being bamboozled. Some of these reviewers hide their paid-for origins by using multiple accounts and IP addresses. I say, go after them, Amazon! This kind of thing ruins the process for everyone.

The trouble came when Amazon appeared to overstep their bounds. I've seen Amazon pull reviews based on flimsy excuses in the past, and so I began to worry.

It is believed that Amazon allows their own sales algorithms to judge a legitimate review based on whether or not the reviewer purchased their review copy directly from Amazon. That is one reason they sometimes tag a review on their site, "Verified Purchase." It is meant as assurance that the reviewer has—at a minimum—bought the book and was therefore likely to have read it.

The trouble with pulling reviews based on purchase is that Amazon may identify a person who has acquired a book legitimately as one of those fake reviewers. That seemed like a good idea at first, but their site is not the only one that sells an item so if their algorithms are not picking up sales of books *not* purchased from them (which would be impossible as nearly as I can tell!), their conclusions may be wrong, terribly wrong. Here is why:

- It is a publishing tradition that publishers and writers provide books at no cost—often special review copies or galleys—to those who write reviews of their book(s). These books would not show up as sales anywhere in Amazon's vast search for fake reviews so they may end up taking innocent reviewers to task.
- Many who write reviews of a book may have received it in real time as a birthday gift or at a holiday party. Even Amazon's digital magic could not record this exchange of property.
- Many reviewers write reviews of books or products that they buy at a bookstore or any other retail outlet and then post them on Amazon. Amazon would have no record of those sales, either.

  Note: Amazon requires those who post reviews have Amazon accounts. That may work as a deterrent, but it has by no means been foolproof.

- Some reviewers may write reviews of books they borrow from the library or buy from secondhand bookstores (including Amazon's!). Those reviewers have as much right to their opinion of a book as anyone. To meddle with a person's first amendment rights may be fraught with more problems than Amazon is willing to take on for this cause.

So, are the bulleted review tactics above indications they are fake reviews? I don't know how Amazon is selecting those people it sues. It *does* appear they have plenty of money to waste if their selection is off base and they lose! Nevertheless, I think they could be on shaky ground once again.

In the meantime, if you review for Amazon (and I think the advantages of doing so are too great to be dismissed easily), avoid touting your own book in the review. The link used in the review (the one that Amazon provides) takes readers back to your profile page. That, dear author/reviewer, should be enough recognition for us. Offering this to authors and reviewers is indeed a gift from Amazon and we should not abuse the hand that feeds us.

If you have read *The Frugal Book Promoter* (bit.ly/FrugalBookPromo), you know that I recommend writing reviews of other authors' books as a way to network and as a way to give back to the industry that makes books possible. In fact, a free and unbiased review is the nicest thing you can give to an author as a token of appreciation and—as an author—it is one of the nicest gifts a reader could possibly give you!

Amazon is one of the best places anyone can post a review. That is where it has the best chance of being read by thousands of readers.

It is important for authors to work at preserving the review tradition that worked so well for us before we were faced with the wild and woolly Internet, but we want to keep

Amazon or anyone else from fingering our reviews as suspect. Here is how Amazon might identify spammy reviewers:

- They may identify related reviewers using IP (Internet Protocol) addresses, the address on the Internet that tells computers where to direct information to your computer. If, Mom, Sis and Dad all use the same computer or e-mail service, Amazon easily identifies them. If someone who is selling reviews uses the same computer for their less-than-ethical business, the IP address they frequent may tattle on them.
- Amazon may identify such reviews by vague, overly gushing, unbalanced reviews. One would presume they might also use similar surnames as an indicator, but that has its own problems. Woe to the Johnsons and Smiths who love books and love to talk about them!
- Amazon may have an oopsy! Technical errors in their algorithms can happen even to tech wonders like the folks at Amazon. When this happens, reviews may disappear and then reappear later.
- Penny Sansevieri, marketing guru at AMarketingExpert.com/, has noticed a correlation between gifting reviewers (or friends and family) with an Amazon Gift Card and the recipients of these cards who then buy your book. Perhaps Amazon suspects the gift card is payment for a review or a bribe. Penny says Amazon finds these gift cards especially suspicious "if the value of the gift card exceeds the cost of the book."

Here are some other things about a review that may cause Amazon and others in the publishing industry to be suspicious or taint the review section of your beautiful buy page:

- Books that have nothing but gushing, five-star reviews may be suspect. Those who know the Amazon review ropes will look for other aspects of the review that point to authenticity. Thus, it is not only unethical for authors to encourage those they query for reviews to assign five stars, it is foolish. It *is* fine to ask for a review. Even to ask for an honest review. It's best not to go beyond that.
- Judging reviews by how short they are seems like an odd way to judge them. It tells us the reviewer is in a hurry, but that is all. Several reviews of my books are one-line reviews and I don't know the reviewer and didn't ask them for a review. I suppose they are just written by nice people who feel compelled to share their opinions, but they may be reviewers who are trying to accrue a great number of reviews to give more credibility to their Amazon status, people who didn't read much, if any of the book. If so, it's a ploy that doesn't reflect well on their ethics or their writing skills.
- Reviews that gush about the superiority of the book can be a tip-off that something is awry but, it is not a conclusive indicator that the review is not the authentic opinion of a reader.
- Reviews that give only one star may be written by people who are competitors or have some other

unspoken agenda. Amazingly, Amazon doesn't seem too concerned about them.

> **Note:** This is not an acceptable way for one author or professional to compete with another. And, luckily, it can backfire.

- Reviews that openly admit they haven't read the whole book because they disagreed with what they found in the first chapter. Or reviews that obviously misinterpret or disrespect an entire work based on one aspect of the book like typos.
- Reviews that seem to have no correlation with the star rating the reviewer gave the book. That could be an indication that it's a paid-for review that promised five stars. Or it might be that the reviewer didn't read the book and therefore cannot support whatever star rating she gave it.
- Amazon's guidelines say reviews shouldn't include "phone numbers; addresses or Web addresses; time-sensitive statements or statements specific to one edition; advertisements or promotions; information on availability, ordering, or shipping; profanity or spiteful remarks; obscene or distasteful content." If a review does this and an author feels the review is also unfair, these violations may be extra ammunition for the author to get the review removed.
- Amazon does not allow professional reviewers (those who are paid for their services) in their "Customer Reviews." That includes paid-for reviews from sought-after review journals but also

reviewers for online review sites that don't pay their reviewers with anything beyond review copies or galleys. Bloggers are not part of this edict, probably because such a rule would be impossible to enforce.

> **Note:** Amazon says, "authors can, however, include [reviews] in the Editorial Reviews section of their book's Product Detail Page." Use your Author Connect (Author Central) page to access this benefit.

It's okay to encourage friends and family to post reviews, but it may be wise to ask them after you have already been successful getting reviews from people who aren't as close to you.

It doesn't take long for an author or new publisher to figure out that asking any reviewer to buy their own review copy may be a deal killer. In any case, it's deemed unprofessional. Reviewers are almost always provided with their review copies at no charge. When you think about it—a lovely ARC or personally signed copy may be the only payment some of these reviewers get. Further, authors certainly don't want to miff the same person who will be judging their book.

Of course, occasionally a reviewer buys a book and then—out of pure generosity—drops by to post a review. They are usually readers who want to share.

What can we do about disappearing reviews? If you encounter disappearing reviews and have a legitimate argument for why they shouldn't be pulled, first double check to be sure the review hasn't moved from its original location in your review queue. If you're sure it is gone, wait a few days to see if a technical glitch was to blame. Sometimes they reappear.

If after a few days' wait the review doesn't magically reappear, contact Amazon's help service through Author Connect. Do not be defensive. Approach the service representative with confidence that Amazon will fix things for you. After all, they are only doing their jobs. My mother used to tell my hard-charging husband that one can "catch a lot more bees with honey than vinegar."

I include these pros and cons so you can make your own decision. You can better argue your case if one or more of your reviews gets pulled—whether it is a review of your book or one you wrote for someone else's book.

MANAGING ALREADY-POSTED REVIEWS

Unless the reviewer has obviously violated one of the guidelines outlined in this chapter, there aren't many things an author can do about it.

Making your case to Amazon may not be something you want to tackle. The likelihood that they will remove a review is slim because they can't violate free speech rights of their reviewers. You may prefer to spend your time doing something more creative and less upsetting than pursuing your case.

But what if you think you have a watertight case that a review should be removed? In that case you can try these courses of action:

- Get busy and query for more reviews. That usually moves the review you dislike down your queue so that it isn't immediately noticed by the reader who is casually browsing. If you need encouragement for this task, think about the many possibilities offered by asking your readers to review your book.
- What if a review said something that is inaccurate or otherwise needs clarifying? You can contact the reviewer and politely point out the errors. If that doesn't work, you can use the comment feature you find at the end of each review. I use this feature sparingly. When you use it, keep your tone positive and let it reflect gratitude for the time the reviewer took to let others know about your book.

> **Note**: I occasionally use the comment feature to thank a reviewer when I can't find a way to thank her with a personal note sent by USPS or by e-mail. I actually prefer to thank hard-to-trace-down reviewers on Twitter, though. It is a show of gratitude to your followers and subtly suggests that they might earn a mention that goes out to your . . . what? 27,000 hard-won and carefully chosen followers.

What about those little "helpful" buttons you see at the bottom of reviews near the comment links on Amazon's review feature? Glad you asked!

- You have a choice to vote helpful (or not).
- Voting "helpful" for reviews is Karma. Vote yes when you can.

> **Tip**: When I thank a reviewer for his or her review, I often tell them, "Of course I rated your review 'helpful.' Good luck with your reviews. Thank you for supporting the publishing industry." Both the thank you and the helpful vote are shows of gratitude, little gifts, and little bonuses in an online world that is often too contentious.

- If your book gets a review that looks dubious—you know, too short or too raving—don't vote for it as helpful. But don't vote as unhelpful, either. You aren't required to put negative energy into the universe.
- A review with a high number of "helpful" votes encourages readers who come to a buy page to read it.
- A review with a high number of positive votes may cause Amazon's algorithm to move it up in the queue so that review is more likely to be read.

> **Tip:** I don't like the idea of an author manipulating the order of reviews by stuffing the Amazon ballot box. Remember that Karma thing. However, authors may encourage readers to vote for reviews as long as they don't tell them how to vote or what to say—or even to influence them. Ethics is a two-way street. If

you win the race for great reviews, you'll feel more successful if they are indeed "fair and honest."

Remember back in the "Getting Started" section of this book when I told you that writing reviews of others' books can be a powerful player in your review-getting program? Let's learn why next. Just as important, let's learn how to get the most benefit from doing so.

Section V
Writing Reviews Are Powerful Platform Builders

"Writing reviews isn't about book sales. It's about building your career . . . and our industry." ~ CHJ

The more an author or a publisher knows about *all* aspects of the review process, the more easily they can use reviews to achieve three very important goals. That is, to get attention for a specific title, to build their writing careers through collaboration and networking, and to use the critiques as a resource for building their writing skills.

When writers review others' books it is Karma. A heartfelt (and honest) review or endorsement is the best gift you can give a fellow author. It benefits other authors, your career, and the industry as a whole.

The process can have benefits, but it can be fraught with danger, too. This section will help you identify pitfalls that lie in wait along the publishing path so you can avoid them. As you tread that path, you'll also learn what works best when you query a reviewer. Knowing these things benefits you, your reviewers, your book, and your career.

Chapter Twelve
Writing Reviews

> "The best gift you can give a writer is a review. Any review! Amazon. Goodreads. Your blog. It follows naturally from the old adage 'Give and ye shall receive.'" ~ CHJ

You're a writer. You already read a lot because reading contributes to the quality of your own writing. So why not write reviews. It doesn't take much more time to write a review for your Web site or blog or for online bookstores after you've finished reading a book. If you don't have time to write full professional reviews, treat them more like casual reader reviews (skipping the usual short synopses, for instance). Keep in mind that writing reviews helps you network. We writers can't expect others to do for us if we aren't willing to do the same—at least occasionally—for other writers.

Here are other advantages:

- You love to write. You love to read. You may love making friends. You need to market your book. Reviewing books helps you do all of those things with very little extra effort.
- About that marketing part. Having your reviews linked to your author page (profile page) on Amazon is a huge advantage.
- The books that you would normally pay for may be free when you write a review.
- You can get books you would normally borrow from the library delivered to your postbox—and you get to keep them.
- You often get to read books you review before the general public gets a crack at them. That gives you an edge over your competitors if you are a professional who writes books in niche markets.
- The bylines and taglines included in your reviews expose your name to a most important audience—people who read books.
- When you write reviews for blogs or other media, you get to include your Web site link in your tagline to improve your site's position on search engines. (If you don't get those benefits, offer your review to another media outlet.)
- Those who read your reviews may follow links in your credits to your online bookstore's buy page.
- Reviewing connects you to the editors and other reviewers at review sites, the same folks who can help you get your book reviewed when the time comes.
- Some reviewers help finance their early writing addiction by writing reviews for paying markets.

- You can earn passive income with your blog and Web site reviews when you embed Amazon's affiliate buy links into the titles of the books you review. Once your affiliate link is embedded, each purchase made on Amazon that is directed to the site from your affiliate link prompts a small finder's fee to your account. Eventually these little fees add up and every little bit helps finance your writing habit.

  Note: To use this Amazon benefit, find the link with the word "affiliate" in it at the bottom of the Amazon home page. Install affiliate links on your blog, Web site, even some of your books.

- If you write articles related to the publishing industry or are a frequent reviewer for a review site or a journal—even if you write them gratis—and your editor is willing to write you a letter of assignment, you may apply to tradeshows like Frankfurt and Book Expo America (BEA) for a press pass. Passes afford you benefits like:
  - Free entry to some publishing and book fair tradeshows, which can translate to considerable savings.
  - That free entry lets you search for opportunities for your book. At the Frankfurt fair, you'll find translators or publishers interested in buying foreign rights to your book, seminars where you can learn more about the publishing industry, and more. If you write books on tech, the

Consumer Electronics Show in Las Vegas offers so many opportunities it will make you dizzy.

o   You will probably have access to the press room where they serve free refreshments and sometimes lunch. That's quite a savings at tradeshows that are usually held in venues where concessions charge above the norm—make that exorbitant prices!—for food.

o   Some let those with press badges place media kits in the tradeshow press room for other reporters and editors to take at will. If you write books about the retail business as I do and you attend retail tradeshows like the Stationery Show held at Javits in New York, your book can be exposed to many other press people interested in the retail industry.

o   Once you become familiar with the way tradeshows work, you might pitch the producers of the show to hire you as a keynote speaker or presenter at seminars.

Tip: Find tradeshows that fit with the topic of your book. Fiction and nonfiction writers should search their books for themes, topics, and related products that might be right for tradeshow networking. It is safe to say that every industry puts on a tradeshow—usually several in the United States and several more internationally.

WRITE GREAT PROFESSIONAL REVIEWS

Writing great professional reviews (as opposed to writing reader reviews) will probably entail tackling a learning curve. It isn't as steep, however, as the curves required when you switch genres from, say, experimental genres to literary or poetry. With a few basic guidelines you can write reviews to be proud of for your blog or other online review entities. Different media outlets have different style guides. Here is a style guide similar to *Midwest Book Review's* guidelines for their reviewers:

- Your review should begin with metadata including:
  - Title.
  - Author.
  - Publisher.
  - Publisher's address.
  - Publisher's Web site address (if they have one).
  - Publisher's e-mail address (if they have one).
  - ISBN.
  - Retail price.
  - Page count.
  - Your name (that would be you as the reviewer).
- To write an engaging review, consider:
  - Including why you selected this particular book for review. Perhaps it relates to your work, hobby, avocation, a particular area of interest, your expertise, or just for fun.

o Adding how the author uses language and structure, illustrates his/her points, develops characters. Use brief quotations from the book to support your observations, opinions, and comments. When writing poetry reviews, include an excerpt from a poem that illustrates a point; when writing a review of a cookbook, include a recipe that appeals to you.

o Who the book is intended for. Address how well the material relates to that audience.

o What is the author is trying to accomplish? Entertain, instruct, persuade, inform, train, teach, alarm?

o Including suggestions for the author to consider next time his or her work appears in print.

o Including a bit about the author's background, credentials, or other titles.

o Including relevant titles that might interest the readers of this book.

Type your reviews in single spaced paragraphs with double spacing between the paragraphs. The review can be a few paragraphs or a few pages—take as much space as you feel is necessary to say whatever you want to say.

Above all, have a good time putting your thoughts and opinions down. The best reviews are those that you would like to listen to while driving along in your car or chatting with friends over lunch. (I interpret this as meaning that this journal would prefer a casual tone rather than too much formality.)

If a book is badly written or not worthwhile, don't write a review. Select another one that you think deserves to be showcased.

> **Hint:** If you plan to pursue reviewing for pay, I recommend you read Mayra Calvani and Anne Edwards' book, *The Slippery Art of Book Reviewing* (bit.ly/BookReviewing) or Magdalena Ball's *The Art of Assessment* (bit.ly/ArtAssessment).

MAKE YOUR REVIEWS WORK FOR YOU

I suspect by now you won't be surprised if I tell you how you can make a good deed—in this case writing reviews for others' books—work for the marketing of your own books.

Do not worry. It's all ethical. It's all part of traditional publishing industry standards. You include bylines and tag lines or credit lines as part of the copy you submit. You know what a byline is. Your name appears under the headline of an article, book title, or whatever, and suddenly those solitary hours sitting in front of a computer make sense. Tag lines or credit lines are the caboose on almost everything you publish, reviews included.

These identifiers are as important as a lunchbox filled with a hearty sandwich is to a railway engineer. Without one he or she would have a tough time maintaining the energy to keep the train moving. These credits are your assurance that if someone wants to communicate with you or offer you an opportunity, they can do it easily. By including them as part of your submissions, they help you control what you would like your audience to know about you and even direct them to the best place to learn more about your book. They also help the author whose book you are reviewing. Because your name is known by many (or soon will be), they add credibility to any review you write.

You know which media use credits and what styles they prefer because you read their submission guidelines and pay attention to the styles of the magazines, newspapers, and Web sites you read. No matter what you write—including reviews—you save your editor the trouble of writing the tagline by submitting your copy the way you'd most like to see it. In doing so, you make her job easier and maintain better control of your own branding.

Your credit line should include your name, the URL or address of your Web site, the name of your book, and a little about you. It's a nice extra to include an e-mail address your readers can use to give you feedback. Many authors maintain a separate e-mail account to accommodate and identify responses generated from their credit lines.

> **Hint:** Rarely seen in taglines is some kind of a hook to encourage the reader to visit your Web site. It might be an offer for a free e-book, a contest, or an intriguing bit of information that will pique the reader's curiosity enough to take action.

Sometimes these credit lines can be expanded to a mini biography. You will have one in your media kit, and to save time you can copy-and-paste it at the end of the reviews where word count is not as important or style guidelines aren't as restrictive. Many bloggers, as an example, love to publish a full paragraph with your review rather than keeping the credit line to twenty-five or fifty words.

Here are two examples, the first a mini bio, the second a shorter tagline. The longer one might be a credit used with an article on a Web site where length is not as important. Notice that information may be mixed and matched to fit with style guidelines for different media and to suit the different titles (genres) an author may write in.

Example of a long tagline or a mini biography:

"Leora Krygier is the author of *First the Raven* (bit.ly/FirstRaven), *When She Sleeps* (bit.ly/WhenSheSleeps), and *Keep Her*, (bit.ly/KeepHerNovel) a young adult novel. She was a finalist in the Ernest Hemingway First Novel Competition the James Fellowship, and the William Faulkner Writing Competition. Lauded for her "linguistic spell" and "poetic prose," Leora is also the author of *Juvenile Court: A Guide for Young Offenders and Their Parents* (bit.ly/JuvenileCourt). She is a referee with the Superior Court of Los Angeles, and has been profiled in the *LA Times* for her innovative use of essay writing in juvenile dispositions. She lives in Los Angeles with her husband and is looking for the perfect poodle to become a member of her family."

Example of a short tagline, the kind that newspapers and periodicals often use:

> Leora Krygier is a juvenile court referee and frequent contributor to magazines for young adults and parents. Reach her at xxxx@aol.com.

Humor and a personal touch can work very well in your credits or biographies.

> **Caveat:** Editors may edit your tagline or may not use it at all. When they publish content you offered at no charge, they should include a tagline or mini bio as a courtesy and probably will if you includ it as part of the copy you submit. If not, politely request that they use one. If they refuse, offer your material elsewhere next time.

Amazon is an exception to the rule for using credit lines with your reviews. Do not include either a byline or credit line. However, when you have an Amazon Author Profile Page, your reviews on the site will link to that page. It's a very nice tradeoff indeed. Check Chapter Nine for information on babying your Amazon Profile Page and Chapter Five where I tell you how to give inexperienced reader reviewers a little help with their reviews.

THE ESSENTIALS FOR GETTING STARTED

Ideas come in strange ways. When you're dreaming. When you're traveling. When you're reading a book like this one. Some seem familiar. Some seem very strange or impossible. Ideas find you, plop themselves in your lap and say "Here I am."

There is a danger—especially when the idea doesn't fit with your original plans—to ignore an idea. As an example, new authors may consider a request for a review from a fellow classmate or critique partner merely a time-eater. If they decline, they may never realize the opportunity they missed.

The trick is to know a little about review resources, outlets, and traditions. That knowledge will give you confidence about whatever direction you go. Will you write an occasional review or will you pursue the possibilities with more vigor?

Whether you are compensated with cash or with exposure for your book, your reviews will be good writing samples and publishing credentials in the future. Don't turn your back on an opportunity until you know what you might be gaining—or losing.

Writing reviews for independent sites and social networks is a good way to perfect your review-writing skills and to build your contact lists. These sites tend to operate on a volunteer basis, but you can network with the other reviewers and the authors whose books you review.

Midwest Book Review often has review opportunities available. To apply as a reviewer, Editor-in-Chief Jim Cox asks you to paste a sample review and a little bio into an e-mail window (not attached) and send it to mwbookrvw@aol.com. Jim says, "Reviewers submitting one review in a given month are posted together in the column 'Reviewer's Choice.' Reviewers submitting two or more reviews in a given month are provided with their own bylined column (e.g. 'Paul's Bookshelf,' or 'Taylor's Bookshelf.'" Here are some other book review sites:

- *Rebeccas Reads* (RebeccasReads.com/) gives very specific guidelines for reviews.
- *MyShelf* (MyShelf.com/) looks for reviewers who offer them exclusives.
- Magdalena Ball's CompulsiveReader.com/ specializes in fiction, especially mainstream literary, and poetry.
- *Book Pleasures* (BookPleasures.com).
- Don't forget to pop your reviews up on sites like BN.com.
- Extend the review you do for any other site by submitting it to my *The New Book Review* (TheNewBookReview.blogspot.com). Submission guidelines are in the left column.

> **Hint:** Lots of the writers and reviewers who use my free service at *The New Book Review* (TheNewBookReview.blogspot.com) don't know how to use a permalink to extend the life of their reviews when they promote it on the Web. To be assured that your reader goes

directly to whatever you are promoting, you use a permalink rather than a general link. It's a courtesy to them and better use of your promotion time. When you post on Blogspot, you'll find a convenient little link icon in the right column of the page. It gives you the permalink to your post even when you are preposting. Just copy, paste and, yesss! Market on social networks to your heart's content! When you submit a review to *The New Book Review*, I send you a more detailed how-to article on using permalinks to promote the review as a thank you for supporting my blog. Submission guidelines are in the left column.

- Don't neglect readers' social networks like LibraryThing.com and Goodreads.com. To increase exposure for your author name, choose sites that appear to attract the most readers in your genre.

  Hint: I developed Reviews for Riters, a model I considered original—if such a thing as original exists. I look for writing techniques the author uses superbly or not so well, ones that emerging authors can emulate—or not. It's a cross between a how-to article and a review. Editors of sites that catered to the needs of writers printed them, and they worked for blogs that attract both readers searching for good books and authors yearning to improve their skills. You might build a niche like this with your own idea.

- You may also post your reviews as videos on bookstore sites like Amazon and on YouTube and their ilk. If you do and it is not forbidden by that site's guidelines, add a subtle ad about your own book and maybe include it as product placement somewhere in the video along with a prominent shot of the book you are reviewing, of course!
- Don't be shy about asking for books you'd like to read; authors and publishers are usually pleased to send you a copy in exchange for a fair and honest review.

> **Hint:** If you cannot recommend a book, don't post a review. That doesn't mean that noting a book's weaknesses isn't valid. It's just that there is no point in slashing and burning a book an author is invested in. Besides, that kind of review isn't likely to help your branding unless the image you are trying to create is that of a curmudgeon.

> **Caveat:** Occasionally an author tries to become a top reviewer. (Amazon lists them as such near the headings of the reviews they post there.) Reaching for this hallowed ground as a means to promote your writing may be an impossible goal because you might spend every waking hour reading and writing about books. Before Harriet Klausner passed away, she had reviewed over 7,000 books. You, I'm sure, would rather write another novel or have a root canal than try to beat her record.

WRITE FOR ONLINE BOOKSTORES

Those who post reviews to online bookstores find they can be networking gold mines and can give their names a new literary luster. Read the submission guidelines. Choose a great title. Edit well. Add a brief tagline but only when it is allowed by the bookstores' guidelines. Always put ethics first or you may be banned from the site. Amazon is the queen of online bookstores so it may be the best site for your reviews though, contrary to belief, you may publish them elsewhere as well. Here are some of the benefits:

- It is a little scary that a review you write on Amazon may easily be read by thousands of readers, but that exposure can benefit your credibility as an author especially if you review books in your genre. Because you are (or will be) a published writer and because these reviews link (or will link) to your author profile page, you want your reviews to reflect your professional status.
- You may work your way up Amazon's review ladder and eventually be invited to be a Vine reviewer. Vine offers these Vine reviewers free books and many other products in the categories they specify—anything from books to jewelry to exercise equipment to household products. In return the reviewer posts a fair and honest review. This privilege is by invitation only. Learn more about using the Vine program for getting reviews for your book in Chapter Nine, "Amazon Can Help Early On, Too."

- Search engine spiders find and list your reviews just about anywhere they appear on the Web; that builds your footprint on Google and other engines quickly.

> **Tip**: Amazon is fussy about their reviews. They have been known to pull some or all of a person's reviews when they do not abide by their guidelines. If you have spent many hours writing reviews, you hope they will expose your own writing to others. Such a loss can feel like a terrible setback. See more on how to avoid some of the problems authors experience with reviews in Chapter Eleven under "When Amazon Reviews Get Yanked."

Don't be dissuaded from writing reviews for Amazon. Misinformation about copyright issues continues to circulate around the Net. If you haven't already heard, the gossip mills churned out by authors (who naturally love to talk) will soon notify you that posting reviews and other content to Amazon makes them Amazon's property and therefore your review cannot be published elsewhere.

I asked Amazon's customer service about their claim to own the material you post to their site. They made it clear that they own only the right to "reuse" what you post, but that you may continue to use the material as you see fit. "Reusing" without pay may not seem like much of an advantage, but when it includes a credit—especially one that includes your book's title and a link back to Amazon's buy page or your Amazon Profile Page—your review becomes free advertising for you.

This explanation of Amazon's policy comes straight from Amazon's customer service department and applies to any of their disclaimers/guidelines that use the term "non-exclusive":

> "When a customer posts . . . to our site, the customer is granting us the nonexclusive right to use the [content]. This means that once [material] is submitted to our site, [it] is ours to use as we see fit for as long as we wish. As this license is non-exclusive, the customer who has written [the material] can also use [their work] as he or she sees fit. The [content] can be included in a book or posted on another site." ~ Nicole L., Amazon.com Customer Service

Authors should be cautious. But they shouldn't reject an opportunity of being read and maybe even discovered based on someone else's bad experience or paranoia.

The downsides to writing reviews should be considered before you make a decision to write reviews to further your writing career. Mary Gannon, Deputy Editor of *Poets & Writers Magazine,* says reviewers take "a lot of heat . . . for some free books, a few bucks, and a byline." However, it's usually only the most famous reviewers who are disparaged for their criticism and only the radical or caustic ones at that.

Many of us worry about lawsuits. We also worry about tax collectors, but authors worry more about tax collectors since the books that reviewers get free must be claimed as taxable income. (Check with your tax accountant.) Neither threat is going to disappear, but you can help protect yourself from both by using a disclaimer in your review. The disclaimer might go something like this:

> "Just so you know, I received a book (or e-book) in exchange for an unbiased and fair review. No fee was charged the author or the publisher."

Here's the nicest thing about making this review-writing decision: You don't have to make a choice. You can have it all. You can write for pay sometimes. You can write reviews to boost your brand sometimes. You can write for authors you know or for authors whose work inspires you. Call the latter the golden-rule choice. The do-unto-others choice. The Karma choice.

WRITE TEN-BEST READS LISTS

Best-reads lists are fun. You get to list your favorite books and that list helps position you as a credible and active part of the literary world. If you happen to write about American history, your list can focus on a topic like the list of "Great American Books" that celebrates the 4th of July in *Time* magazine (July 11, 2016 issue). You can assemble a general list, of course, but the reader attracted to your brand is more likely to be attracted to a list that relates to your book. Your fans will come to expect your list (even rely on it!) if you do one regularly. You'll double its clout if you can relate your list to a season or holiday.

Ten-best reads lists can be a vital part of your review writing effort. They can be published by you and republished by bloggers and other media. Later, as your writing career develops (and the time you can alot to reviewing diminishes), they can substitute for reviews—perhaps garner even more online attention.

Many online review sites like MyShelf.com ask their reviewers to assemble these lists as a once-a-year feature they can promote. I found Magdalena Ball, my poetry partner for our Celebration Series of Chapbooks (bit.ly/CarolynsPoetryBooks), when she included my first book of poetry published by Finishing Line Press on her site's "Top Reads" list. (By the way, a thank-you note for that much-appreciated gesture was part of what lead to our networking success story!)

Here are other benefits of writing ten-best lists:

- You might let your lists do double or triple duty (and save you time) by posting them on Goodreads, your blog, or a site you write reviews for.
- You'll get links to your Web site or online buy page in the biography or credit. The credit line for your list will, of course, include information like your name, your book's title, a smart pitch for your book, and a link where a reader can buy your book. These links always add something to your search engine exposure and sometimes lead to other opportunities.
- You may get money or merchandise credits from affiliate programs mentioned earlier in the chapter if you use them regularly. Search for "making Amazon affiliate links" to learn more about the affiliate program Amazon offers. It's free and takes

less than a minute to produce once you have mastered your first one. (There is a link to that affiliate function at the bottom of Amazon's home page—in very small font.)

- When you let authors know you included their title on your ten-best list, you are networking at the highest level. Make an effort to keep in touch with those authors through your social networks. They may someday be willing to return the favor in some way—perhaps a review of your next book.
- When social networks link to your ten-best list on Twitter and other social networks, you get additional exposure for your brand.
- Books you purchase can be taken as a business expense on your taxes if you itemize expenses.

There are, of course, other ways you can be of service or return favors to authors. You can tweet their blurb and book cover images or tell your Facebook friends about books you have read and liked. You can attend a fellow author's book signing or launch party and take a picture to post on Instagram or your Facebook page.

Now it's time to get motivated—to write those reviews that can do so much for your book and get more ideas for doing so. It's onward and upward.

.

Section VI
Onward and Upward

"There are plenty of reasons to be proud. Write them down. If you don't celebrate the small wins, you don't have much to build on. It's all about momentum."
~ Joyce Jilson, astrologer

Many years ago, I happened across the above advice for my zodiac sign from Joyce Jilson whose prescriptions for success appeared in my daily newspaper. It doesn't matter whether it was intended for Leos, Aries, or Sagittarians because it is perfect for all writers any day of the year.

It seems our achievements are never enough because success demands more success. It seems creative people are especially success-myopic; we don't see it when it comes along and perches itself in our laps. It's so easy to be infected by negativity—the news about everything from war to the state of publishing is just so dreadful. This section helps you get a grasp on those negative feelings—especially less-than-desirable feelings about reviews—and turn them into actions that will propel your book and writing career onward and upward.

Chapter Thirteen

Your Reviews, Media Kit, and Visualizing the Future

> "The greatest benefits of writing and publishing a book are the skills and confidence you build in the process." – CHJ

If you disparage your own achievements, you are not alone. People who do that have trouble building confidence to try for more or better. Promotion successes kick start a cycle of success only if we put them to use for us psychologically. It's dangerous for your promotion efforts (and your writing) not to nod in the mirror at your victories—large and small.

An online coaching company for business people who need help with their presentations tells their visitors to "Visualize yourself succeeding." Short, sweet, and fine advice. Rhonda Byrne has become one the most successful writers around advising people to use techniques that have been known for a very long time, things like the law of attraction and manifestation. It's all about attitude. Her attitude certainly helped her *NY Times* bestseller, *The Secret* (bit.ly/RhondasSecrets), succeed.

Sometimes we don't celebrate or visualize success because we don't recognize when we have achieved it. Was "success" that first royalty check? Will "success" only come when our book's name appears on *The Times* bestseller list? Was it the day we started commanding $5 a word as a freelancer? Or are these all mirages that are expunged by insecurity once we have achieved them?

The easiest way to recognize success is to write down goals. Once they're in black and white, more recent expectations can't muss up our perspective. We'll know when we deserve to celebrate. Remember when you thought you'd never get a book written? That day is here. That *is* success.

What if the goal you jot down is "to be just like Danielle Steele?" Study her technique. Take classes. Then tap into your own originality. You may not want to *be* the great D.S., but many of us want to have our voices recognized as hers is. When I feel less than successful, I reread *Word Works* (bit.ly/WordsthatWork) by Bruce Holland Rogers. It's perceptive, witty, perfectly written. Have you heard of him? He won several awards including the Nebula (sfwa.org/). He is an example that even if you are big in all the ways that count, your name may not be a household word. So if our names aren't famous, will we still feel we have no value? Probably. Unless we've made a list of those goals and celebrate each time we get to cross one off our list.

So what about the process of writing down goals—and then writing down achievements even if they *weren't* originally part of our goals? I use my virtual media kit for recording achievements in sections like "Published Works" and "Speaking and Appearances." (The ones that are unnecessary for a particular marketing duty can easily be removed now that we have digital magic for cutting and pasting!)

When I teach a workshop on producing our own media kits, I ask my attendees to step away from the online world they have become accustomed to and back into the hands-on world. As an educator, I know that tactile experience stays with us a long time—sometimes longer than visual or auditory. So, I have them bring a stack of folders or folded papers that we pretend are real live folders and—by extension—represent the folders in your computer. We label each one as a section we will use in our media kits. Some of them will actually turn out to *be* sections of our media kit (after we have reworked them, edited them, and formatted them). But others are just lists of our successes that can be used over time as resources when our careers require that we revisit a certain aspect of our pasts or just as memory-joggers when we need an upper.

For purposes of this book, I encourage you to imagine (or make) a real folder that tracks reviews and reviewers. Yes, it turns out that the best and most prestigious of the entries in this folder will be part of your permanent kit. Be sure to stick in dates and the title of the book each reviewer reviewed for you. If you have only one book now, visualize how much more useful this folder will be later when you have two or a dozen.

I'm sure you can see how valuable tracking your successes like this can be for your future. If you want step-by-step instruction for your entire kit, check the index of your copy of *The Frugal Book Promoter* (bit.ly/FrugalBookPromo) for "media kits" and read all the entries there. You will come away with a media kit that can be sent to the major review journals that request books or manuscripts before their release dates. And you'll use your kit for a whole lot of other things, too!

Rachel Maddow, anchor and pundit at MSNBC and author in her own right, says we can build confidence by pretending. Twelve step programs use a similar approach they call "acting as if." When we do that, our demeanor (think "perceived authority") builds. That is the onward and upward path. From getting reviews to everything else in our careers—and in life.

In this chapter I mentioned Rhonda Byrnes book, *The Secret* (bit.ly/RhondasSecrets). In it she suggests you use a visualization board. Put it where you can see it from your work area and post all the things you wish for on it—preferably in a visual way. When you look at it, think about future successes as if they are happening right now. In this moment. The onward and upward start taking care of themselves when you believe it.

Chapter Fourteen
Getting Questions Answered *à la* Ann Landers

"There is only one thing better than learning from our own mistakes. It's learning from the booboos, blunders, and gaffes of others." ~ CHJ

So, dear reader, what if you didn't get it right the first time! What if you feel frozen or depressed about an aspect of your review process? If you've read this book through, you probably suspect I don't much like being told no or that there is only one right way to do something. It is part of my onward-and-upward-with-no-delays philosophy.

That's one reason I love Q&A formats; they tend to highlight alternative views. That love comes, in part, from some of my first experiences as a journalist. The editor at my first "real" paid writing job put me to work making Ann Landers' columns fit into space allotted on page layouts the advertising and backshop departments had designed for the section that was then called "Society." It's the money that comes from advertising that keeps newspapers alive so *they* get first dibs on the space. Sometimes there was not enough room for all of Ann's letters so it was my duty to edit, cut, and fix so they fit and were still intelligible.

In the process, I learned a lot from the letters about life's little problems including roadblocks similar to the ones we run into with reviews. Q&As are an easy way to identify problems and to make them easily understandable because they are anecdotal. So, you are going to get a few short Q&As that answer some questions about the review process that keep you awake at night. Sometimes they are questions about specifics, sometimes general. But they are exercises in learning from one another. All are adaptations of actual Q&As *à la* Ann Landers that I use in my newsletter (bit.ly/SWWNewsletter) and in the seminars I teach.

How can I get reviews for my print book if I published it as an e-book first?

QUESTION: I published a book only as an e-book about a year ago. I want to make it available in print. Given its prior availability as an e-book, would review journals still be interested in reviewing it? I've looked at a few submission guidelines but none speak directly to that point.

ANSWER: Never say never! Although the major review journals' deadlines have long since passed for your book, go back to Chapter Six for my back-door method of getting reviews even after submission deadlines have passed. It may suggest ways for authors to circumvent other annoying situations, too.

Unless having major journals review your book is a big-time dream of yours, I'd rather see you use alternative methods for getting large numbers of reviews instead of focusing on the prestigious review journals. Because of the Web, reviews almost never become dated, and, taken cumulatively, their reach to new readers may be infinitely greater than those big-journal reviews we struggle to get. You can continue to link to your online reviews until you publish a new edition . . . or until you kick the bucket.

You didn't say how long the e-book has been available. If it hasn't been long, a journal may decide that the delay is not significant. Be sure to make that point in your query letter. Please find my list of the big journals on my Web site at bit.ly/GetEthicalReviews.

Help! I don't want to risk sharing my work!

QUESTION: I want to take a class at my local university but I'm afraid if I let someone else—even the instructor— see my manuscript they'll steal my idea. Should I have a lawyer draw up an agreement for protection?

ANSWER: Teachers, agents, publishers and other publishing professionals—even editors—find a persistent misconception among new authors. They believe they shouldn't share their manuscript with others before it is published and copyrighted. I've seen it frequently among my students at UCLA. They are so secretive they don't want their instructors or fellow students (who are in a position to both critique and give blurbs and reviews) a peek at their idea. This attitude, of course, severely limits their ability to get a book published—to get everything from informed publishing advice to a foreword for their book. Waiting for proofs of a book or confirmation from the copyright office eliminates many of an author's best hopes for great support from others early in the publishing game.

Furthermore, the distrust shown by presenting these associates with legal papers may cause them to tactfully tell you they are unavailable for help rather than coach you through your paranoia. Worse, you may never know why they weren't open to your request and so you continue to discourage experts who could be instrumental in your success.

Going the legal route can be done, of course. Just know that you may be doing yourself a disservice and that there is no such thing as copyrighting an *idea*, anyway. Thank goodness. If they hadn't, Shakespeare would be considered a plagiarizer and there would be no such thing as science fiction because many of those ideas are borrowed from physics. A recent case in London made that a certainty. For more reassurance on copyright and a little about the writing exercise my critique group used to prove this point, see Chapter Four in this book.

The wary (and everyone else!) should determine who the professionals are. That may take some research. I tend to trust those who have been vetted by accredited universities and those referred by others I have grown to trust. It seems like a good middle ground. And, yes. Of course I copyright my published work.

Am I dreaming or does Amazon have double standards for reviews?

QUESTION: I am not so concerned about getting reader reviews for my book on Amazon as I am about Amazon's double standard regarding the way they enforce their review guidelines for books published by independent authors and small presses and those published by big publishers. It's especially egregious when Amazon removes reviews that violate their guidelines.

ANSWER: A noted author of several how-to books about how to negotiate different aspects of the Amazon morass noted that "Amazon goes on binges of enforcing guidelines, often overdoing it and then falling back to benign neglect." The get-tough sprees often come after Amazon has received some bad publicity so that expert thinks the "double standard observation" may be more a matter of timing than singling out specific publishing models.

That indie authors often depend on asking personal friends and relatives to post reviews—especially for those first reviews—contributes to this belief. Amateur reviews are less likely to read or heed the guidelines or understand the review process in general and many of the things they do tend to trigger Amazon's built-in alarm system. Please refer to Chapter Three for more on book bigotry (because it still does exist!) and Chapter Twelve for ways to help these reviewers avoid these pitfalls.

I'm scared that Amazon will retaliate if I say something negative about them.

QUESTION: I have some gripes about Amazon but am hesitant to let my fellow authors know about them because I fear some backlash from a very powerful entity in the publishing world.

ANSWER: The same acknowledged expert I quoted above says, "It is unlikely that Amazon pays attention. No one would remember or notice. Unless your [opinions] show up in *The New York Times*, [Amazon is] very impersonal."

I want to ask for endorsements without sounding like a telemarketer.

QUESTION: My coaching client says, "I'm striking out with blurb requests from my personal contact list. I am wondering about the etiquette of e-mailing writers who don't know me yet. For instance, authors whose books were helpful for my research but with whom I have not previously interacted online. I don't want to seem presumptuous, like a cold-calling telemarketer!"

ANSWER: Sure it's okay. Just be sure you mention that you used their books for your research (or however else you came to know them) and be very specific so your letter doesn't look like a blanket template. If you can cite a reason you appreciated their work, so much the better.

After you've done that, you can pitch your request for an endorsement or blurb. You will find it helpful if you resurrect your copy of my *The Frugal Editor* (bit.ly/FrugalEditor) and read the sections on query letters and agents' pet peeves. There are lots of little things to do and to avoid in that chapter—things that aren't necessarily wrong, just unprofessional, boring, or irritating to those in the industry because they are overused. Of course, no one ever gets tired of hearing that their book has been useful or that they are trusted or that they have credibility.

How much reminding—or pestering—is allowed?

QUESTION: My coaching client Jendi Reiter, author of *Two Natures* (bit.ly/JendiReiter), says, "A couple of years ago I won a fiction contest from a well-known literary magazine judged by a prominent author. Now I would like to solicit him for a blurb for my forthcoming novel. The journal agreed to forward my blurb request to him two months ago but I have not heard from him since. Is it appropriate for me to send a second message to big-name authors who have not responded to my first contact? Should I resend another message through one of these contacts on his Web site? Should I send it to the media inquiries e-mail at his publisher's address or the bookings e-mail at his agent's address?

ANSWER: Yes. It is fine to recontact someone. And it's not just me who says that. I originally heard it from agent Michael Larson when we were both presenting at a writers' conference. He was amazed at how many authors don't follow up on initial contacts. Your book *is* your business now and one is expected to monitor efforts in the business world. For your second approach, cushion your request by saying something like, "I am contacting you again because I fear there may have been a digital snafu along the way or that my request inadvertently didn't get forwarded to you."

You can also try sending the request via USPS directly to his agent's office or his publisher's office. His satellite associates are more likely to forward a letter posted to him that way. They may do so without even opening it.

If you have no luck with one of these methods, try e-mail again a few weeks later. You may even be able to reach him via Twitter with a direct message. Publicist Penny Sansevieri says, "Everyone is equal on Twitter!"

It does seem logical to try an alternative rather than using the same media inquiries or bookings e-mail addresses you tried before.

Wahhh! Celebrities don't have time to review or endorse.

QUESTION: My upcoming book discusses topics that are in the news today. I have tracked the names of celebrities and government officials who have spoken about these issues in the media. A review from one of them would be wonderful, but I doubt they would take the time to read it. How would you proceed?

ANSWER: Your question points to the grief that authors (especially new authors) experience when they try to get reviews. The biggest mistake you are making is underestimating the value of your book. The second is supposing the only way to appeal to these influencers is to ask for reviews. There are other ways to do it. You might ask them to write a foreword. Or you might ask them for a blurb or endorsement.

The key to approaching someone with a request is showing them how they (or the cause they have been speaking out about) might benefit. The other is to make it as easy as possible for them to help you.

I mentioned my husband's persistence in pursuing endorsements for his *What Foreigners Need to Know about America from A to Z* (amzn.to/ForeignersAmericaUS) earlier in this book. To get reviews he solved the "time to read it conundrum" for his very thick book by copying the first page of each of his twenty-six chapters so his contacts could get the gist of his book without seeing the entire manuscript. He did offer them the full manuscript if they preferred.

Lance's method worked but he had even better luck asking for an endorsement (many outside the publishing world have no idea what a "blurb" is). He duplicated his successful use of first-page overview, but also included a couple of suggested blurbs they could use with reminders that they could adapt any one of them to better fit the message they would like to highlight, use any one of them as it was written and send it back to him with their permission to use it, or write their own using the endorsements as a guide.

The results he got were amazing. They included ambassadors from the US to China and China to the US, famous journalists in India and more. Many took the time—contrary to his expectations—to write their own endorsements. He, of course, made sure that each of them received a book of their own as a thank you once it was in print.

One of my husband's favorite quotes comes from Emily Dickinson. She said, "Hope is the thing with feathers / That searches the soul / And sings the tune without the words / And never stops . . . ." He says what he got from that now he is an author is to use that hope to propel us to risk doing what we think is right for our books.

Chapter Fifteen

When Your Book Sales Get Musty

"About Publishers: I conducted a study (employing my usual controls) that showed the average shelf life of a trade book to be somewhere between milk and yoghurt." ~ Calvin Trillin, humorist

Milk and yoghurt, indeed! There is now—metaphorically speaking—a new kid on the block who will help you keep your book on the charts as long as you want it there.

You guessed it. The new kid is the new breed of bloggers and reader reviewers. This chapter is about how you can perk up sales using what you learned in this book about reviews, and it includes a couple of aids not mentioned before to add to your review-getting tool box. If this prospect doesn't set you on fire, consider that this continuing effort for your last book may propel your next one—and your next—to greater heights.

FIGHT THE IT'S-TOO-LATE URGE

Let's say your book has been out a year. You are ready to write another book. You don't think your promotion is working. You think you've missed your chance.

I can't tell you how many authors I've seen give up on flinging promotion stones into their marketing pond about the time they would have started to see results if they had stuck with it.

Publicity is like the little waves you make when you toss pebbles into a lake. The waves travel, travel, travel and eventually come back to you. If you stop lobbing stones, you lose momentum. The marketing you continue to do builds your career. Getting reviews is one of the best career-builders; it helps you keep in touch with old contacts in the industry, and the review process provides the longest lasting results now that the Web offers findability well beyond the time the most influential paper journal or newspaper is relegated to a bookshelf or a recycle bin.

Book reviews are your forever-after-the-launch marketing tool. Here's why planning another major review-getting campaign (or adding reviews at a slow and steady rate as demonstrated by the tortoise in Aesop's fable) is so darn effective:

- When your next book comes out, your first review will still be up on Amazon complete with the battery of reviews you have worked so hard to get.

- That search engine footprint you built using reviews won't disappear.
- New books build on the momentum of old books. New reviews keep that momentum from flagging.
- You keep building your contact list of reviewers for the future.
- New reviews keep your name in places where old readers will be reminded of you and new readers begin to recognize your name.

Don't let tried-and-true processes go stale just because you are writing a new book. Here's how:

- Add new reviewers' e-mail addresses to your media list.
- As you run across new reviewers, don't wait until you have a new book with a new copyright date to act. Ask them to review your previous book now. They will be more receptive to your next book, even if they decline this review.
- Stay in touch with old reviewers with the methods we discussed in Chapter Ten.
- When you or your book are honored with an award or in some other way related to the publishing industry, let your reviewers know about it.
- Tailor query letters for your new book so the reviewer remembers you from the review she did for your last book. This time ask for an interview or offer her a guest blog post—perhaps an excerpt from your one of your previous books that includes a credit touting your new book.

- When you have new book-related news to shout out with a media release, introduce it with a personal paragraph so recipients are aware they gave you publicity when your first book was released or when they reviewed your first book.
- Run a review contest on your Web site, on Twitter, at Goodreads or in your newsletter. Old books never go out of style, especially if they are free.
- Some of your reviews (both others' reviews of your book and reviews you've written about others' books) have begun to age from disuse. Start posting them (with permission from the reviewer) on Web sites that don't demand exclusives. Check the guidelines for my free review service blog in the left column of *The New Book Review* (TheNewBookReview.blogspot.com).
- Send notes to friends and readers you know have read your book. Ask them to recommend your book to others, write an endorsement for you, or review your book. One of those things at a time, though. Stay focused. Let them know how it will help you and let them know you appreciate their support.

One of my favorite sayings is, "For marketing to work, you have to promote the promotion." That is true of reviews no matter where they have found a home. Link to them and keep networking those links on social networks like Twitter. When you do that, you're doing your book, your career, and your reviewer a favor.

Rekindle your marketing campaign with something you haven't tried before. That might mean you have to learn something new, but what's the fun in the same old stuff? Try these:

- Learn to use quick response codes (QRs) if you  aren't already using them. Some people think QR codes look flowery . . . or like puzzles or computer chips . . . even Rorschach tests. They are a kind of barcode, but they can take people with smartphones to a Web page or video or even make a call for them—it depends on what the author chooses to put in the code. You might lead people to the review page on your Web site or to a reviewer's blog using the specific permalink that takes them directly to your review. Display QRs at book fairs, tradeshows, and book signings to let folks with smart phones scan whatever promotional gift or information you want them to have. You can put them anywhere: Your business cards, your ads, in your book, or on your printed tote bag. The leading maker of codes is Scanbury. Related to them is a program called Scanlife. Get free codes made at several sites. The example you see here takes you to the Writers' Resources pages on my Web site.

- Google Alerts has been around a long time, but authors often don't use it or a similar tool for finding new reviewers often enough. I use it to inform me when my name or titles have appeared anywhere on the Web so I can comment and send thanks. It's also useful for those who are doing research for a book by letting them know when pertinent keywords are mentioned anywhere on the Web. Find the Google Alerts service on your Google account page. Look for the little bell icon.

- Check out online services that help you promote e-books. Most require that you have a certain number of reviews. By now you probably have enough. Many of these services are free. E-mail me for a list of these services at HoJoNews@AOL.com. Put GETTING GREAT REVIEWS: E-BOOK PROMOTION LIST in the subject line. Two I like are AskDavid.com and AwesomeGang.com. They are different from one another, but I found their free services effective for marketing other book promotions. Use great excerpts from your reviews as part of the copy you give to them.

- Take up a new habit that will nudge Amazon's algorithms like using the social network icons located on your book's buy page. Using them instead of going directly to the social networking pages to update your status will make Amazon's algorithms sit up and take notice.

   Tip: When you use Amazon's Twitter icon like this, edit the suggested tweet that pops up so it reflects features one of your briefest blurbs.

CATALOGS ARE RARELY USED JUGGERNAUTS

Commercial catalogs—you know, the kind you find in your mail box and sometimes your e-mail box—benefit from the great blurbs you have excerpted from your reviews. In fact, you are more likely to get a contract for your book to be featured in a commercial gift or product catalog if you have a great review and have excerpted stunning blurbs. The catalog's designers can use them to prompt their readers to buy your book. And, wow! Are these catalogs a way to pick up musty book sales!

Catalogs are show business. They spotlight a product for the purpose of selling merchandise, but they also create a buzz, project an image, tell a story, leave an impression. They create celebrity for themselves and for each of their products.

Brick-and-mortar stores and online retailers of every kind—from department stores to gadget stores to catalogs for seniors—send catalogs by USPS and by e-mail. Millions of them.

Before authors or publishers pitch a book to one of these catalogs, they must find a catalog-match for the genre, theme, or topic of their book. Here are a few examples of how books can add a new dimension to catalogs:

- Your nonfiction book on the life of Picasso or your historical fiction account of his life is a great prospect for a catalog produced by art galleries like Smithsonian or the New York Metropolitan Museum of Art.
- Your how-to travel book or travel-oriented memoir will fit on the pages of *Travelsmith.*

- Your nonfiction book on precious stones may fit a high-end catalog featuring reproductions of the elaborate—and famous—eggs designed by Fabergé for Czars Alexander III and Nicholas II to give to their wives as Easter gifts. Your historical fiction book set in Czarist Russia would be a nice addition to the same section of that same catalog.
- Your book on the history of porcelain or bone china could be featured in *Geary's* catalog. Geary's is an ultra-fine gift store located on Rodeo Drive in Beverly Hills, so a fiction book set in that area or about a Beverly Hills lifestyle might give their catalog a dimension they haven't tried before.

Once you find a match, pitch your idea with the query-letter basics described in Chapter Six. This query, however, must emphasize why this book is a fit for this catalog buyer's publication and how she might best showcase it. Use your best short blurb as the clincher to your pitch. Because catalogs need great visuals, include an image (not as an attachment) of your knockout cover.

Here's how to find catalogs that might be interested in your book:

- Search online for "retail catalogs." About 14,000,000 lists and individual catalogs will appear. Narrow the search to include only catalogs for which your book is a fit.
- Go to a bookstore or library and ask to see their *Catalog of Catalogs*. Find one or more categories that fit your book. Tada! You've found another way

to see your book cover and your blurbs in print and realize sales at the same time.

- Become familiar with the catalogs that come to your home. Ask your friends to share their used catalogs with you. When you find an appropriate one for your book, go for it! Contact information is usually on the inside of the front cover or on the back cover.

The benefits of these kinds of retails sales far exceed those of selling retail through bookstores:

- The primary reason for your book to appear on the pages of a retail catalog is sales, but that exposure is also extraordinarily good publicity.
- Though commercial catalog exposure looks like advertising, it has more benefits than most ads. Here's the best part: It is not usually exposure you pay for. The catalog administrators buy books from you and do all of the production and distribution work. Your only job is to sell them on the idea of your book, provide them with ideas for copy including one of your book's rave reviews, and send them a great image of your book, perhaps a 3-D image, which you can get from Gene Cartwright at ifogo.com/3dchj/ if you don't know how to do it on your own.
- Catalog buyers reorder just before their stock is depleted, usually with no prompting from you or your publisher.
- Unlike most bookstores or other retail outlets, print catalog companies expect to pay the freight for their book shipments.

- Unlike most bookstores, catalog producers do not return what they cannot sell. They probably won't ask for returns unless you suggest it, and why would you do that? This is their usual way of doing business. When in Rome, do as the Romans do.

  Hint: These no-return sales terms should be included on order forms, invoices, and the sales contract.

- Catalog buyers must be sure they have stock to cover their sales, so their orders will be substantial enough to make both you and your publisher smile.
- If catalog sales are successful, administrators may ask for a contract for their *next* catalog. The beauty here is that you can help make sales soar by promoting the catalog on Twitter, your newsletter, and many of your other marketing efforts. Use the motto "As seen in Smithsonian's Holiday Catalog!" everywhere.
- Commercial catalogs expect you to set minimum quantities of what you sell them. That means you can tell them—as an example—that their minimum first order must be forty-eight books and orders thereafter must be in lots of at least six or twelve. I'm sure you can see the benefits of this policy, not least of which is that they will be less likely to run out of stock. You'll save on accounting time, too.
- If, after the catalog has expired, you can coax the administrators of these catalogs to share their graphics with you, you can repurpose them for your Web site and about any other place great graphics will help your marketing. They probably won't charge you if you

make it clear that you intend to keep using their catalog in your marketing. Depending on how the segment is designed, it might become a logo, a banner for your social networks, and on and on.

- Catalogs usually don't care if the copyright date on your book is current; they are more interested in a title that fits their product mix, has a history of great sales, and has appealing cover art.
- Most catalogs don't require exclusivity for their products.
- You might interest some online catalogs to buy rights to *give* your e-book to their customers as a value-added gift for a limited period of time.

> **Note:** Many small-to-medium size publishers have no experience with catalogs and, though it seems self-evident that increased sales benefit them as well as you, you may need to convince them of that fact and then coach them through the process.

Catalog disadvantages are:

- Learning curve ahead! You'll need to expertly pitch your book and negotiate sales to catalog buyers. That means you have to readjust your thinking and tailor your sales tools to their needs. As you can see from the bullets in the list above, catalogs do business differently from bookstores.
- Because print catalogs buy products in quantity and in advance they demand a hefty discount. If you or your publisher cannot give fifty percent or more, there is no point in pursuing them. However, if you

only break even on catalog sales, it may be worth the trouble for the publicity benefits.

> **Note:** When you make your calculations remember that the catalog pays shipping costs as mentioned above.

- Some authors and publishers fail to print enough books to supply a catalog's immediate needs. Authors and publishers who use print-on-demand technology have the advantage of fast turnaround time, something a partner- or self-published author may use as a sales point in his or her query letter.
- Nonfiction books are generally more suitable for catalogs, but as with other marketing, anything that works for nonfiction may work for fiction, too. It may just take more research and planning to achieve success.

> **Hint:** It's hard to believe that some publishers don't jump at the chance to work with their authors on catalog sales. If your publisher can't be convinced of the profit possibilities in partnering with you on a project like this, handle the details of this sale yourself. Ask your publisher for a large-quantity price break to stock your own books or work with the press that prints your book so you can save postage and time by having catalog orders drop-shipped.

Authors can produce catalogs of their own. Self-published catalogs are generally sponsored or organized by authors with independent instincts who have the support of charitable and professional organizations including writers' organizations.

> **Tip:** Don't let that "self-published catalogs" scare you. Authors who are traditionally published can use this idea as effectively as those who have had experience publishing their own work.

These independently-produced catalogs become cross-promotional efforts that increase exposure for holiday gift-giving. They are great promotional handouts at literary events. They are take-it-home marketing tools that continue to sell after attendees have returned home. And they can be targeted at any demographic.

When Joyce Faulkner and I sponsored a booth for Authors' Coalition at the LA Times Festival of Books we published a full-color catalog that featured all our booth participants. We handed them out at the fair, but we also mass-mailed them to influential creative people in the Southern California area including Hollywood movie moguls who often adapt novels for the screen. We didn't forget to include regional bookstore buyers and event planners, and the fair logo gave it even more credibility. (Fair administrators encouraged fair participants to use the logo liberally.) The catalog included an invitation to come to the fair and visit our booth. And, yes—because blurbs are superior sales tools—a quote excerpted from reviews was featured prominently on each author's page.

Cooperative catalogs benefit by linking to great reviews of each book. When this is part of the concept, those online entities (bloggers, journals, etc.) may be thankful enough for the additional traffic to help with the catalog's digital marketing—things like social networking and blog posts.

To achieve mass readership, catalogs like this rely on participating authors to distribute it to their own contact lists. All benefit from each author's list. E-mail distribution is thrifty, but paper catalogs are keepers and can be distributed as giveaways at events or through the mail. You can use the catalog images in slide shows for YouTube and Web sites to encourage people to subscribe to receive next year's catalog.

When individuals or organizations spearhead catalogs like this, there is usually a fee to cover the time and expense of putting them together and for coordinating the dissemination. They can be used as fundraisers for charities or to help a small publisher increase their bottom line so they can take on more publishing clients the following year.

> **Note:** Make an idea like this work by asking participants to sign agreements that clearly delineate the marketing needed by each participant and the duties of the organizing entity.

Congratulations! You can now do what you might otherwise pay someone else to do and make the most of worthwhile review-getting services, too. Come back from time to time for inspiration and to refresh your review getting skills.

Appendices

"Appendices were invented by elves who delight in keeping trade secrets tucked away where only the most curious readers find them." — CHJ

Appendices can be full of obscure resources, strict rules, and templates. When I interviewed literary agents for the chapters on query letters in my multi award-winning *The Frugal Editor* (bit.ly/FrugalEditor), Stephanie Kip Rostan, an agent for Levine/Greenberg Literary Agency, Inc., said, " . . . don't slavishly follow a query letter template . . . . If you can't write a query letter on your own, I have to be concerned about your ability to write a book. Besides, it's just creepy."

Your book is like no other. Each publishing occasion that calls for a query—anything from a request for representation to an appeal for a TV appearance—is different. Ditto for each circumstance that requires a media release. Thus, the samples (templates?) in my appendices are merely suggestions. Still, the more you know about all the processes involved in marketing and the publishing industry, the greater your chance for success. The more you know about the "rules," the more confident you will be when you need to break one of them.

Use the samples I provide in these appendices as guides so you don't stray into embarrassing territory. Use the suggested reading to expand your awareness of the publishing industry's possibilities. But in the long run, it is *your* voice and the ambience of each circumstance that dictates how anything in these appendices should be used.

SUGGESTED READING

The books listed below are my personal recommendations and, where possible, contain links to an online bookstore or to the author's Web site. In addition to considering their content, I recommend books that are fun and easy to read. Learning more about writing needn't be drudgery!

For Career Building

- *Writer's Market Deluxe Edition 2016* (bit.ly/WritersMarket) includes a one-year subscription to Writer's Digest Web site.

   Tip: *Midwest Book Review* guarantees reviews for the first-place winners of all Writer's Digest's contests. *Midwest's* reviews are open to all books regardless of the press they are published on but generally a review isn't guaranteed.

On Book Proposals

- My *The Great First-Impression Book Proposal* (bit.ly/BookProposals) takes only about thirty minutes to read. You don't need to read a tome or several books because the guidelines in this booklet make it easy for you to write a professional book proposal, one that also makes it easy for editors to see how valuable your proposed book can be.

If for some reason you still don't feel secure about your proposal, try one of these full-length books:

- *Book Proposals That Sell: 21 Secrets to Speed Your Success* at webmarketingmagic.com/app/?af=615838 by Terry Whalin.
- *How to Write a Book Proposal* (Writer's Digest) by Michael Larsen at bit.ly/MichaelLarsen.
- Patricia Fry's new *Propose Your Book: How to Craft Persuasive Proposals for Nonfiction, Fiction, and Children's Books* (bit.ly/PatriciaFry) tackles proposal for specific genres.

On Editing and Revision

A true edit is not only about typos. It's about everything including structure, and it sometimes requires a rewrite. Sorry, but that's the way writing can be in its bluest moments. I look for books that give practical, easily understood help:

- The second edition of my *The Frugal Editor: From your query letters to final manuscript to the marketing of your new bestseller* (bit.ly/FrugalEditor).
- *Don't Murder Your Mystery* (bit.ly/ChristRoerden) by Chris Roerden.
- *Story Fix* (bit.ly/BrooksStoryFix) by Larry Brooks.
- *Writing Dialogue* (bit.ly/Chiarella) by Tom Chiarella. Published by Writer's Digest.
- My *Great Little Last-Minute Editing Tips for Writers: The Ultimate Frugal Booklet for Avoiding Word Trippers and Crafting Gatekeeper-Perfect Copy* (bit.ly/Last-MinuteEditing).

Also see the "On Grammar" suggestions in the section below even if you pulled down As in English when you were in high school.

On Reviews

- *The Art of Assessment* (bit.ly/ArtAssessment) by Magdalena Ball.
- *The Slippery Art of Book Reviews* (bit.ly/BookReviewing) by Mayra Calvani and Anne K. Edwards. Published by Paladin Books.

On Grammar and Style

Notice I'm not recommending the usual sources for grammar like Strunk and White. That book has been confusing students and writers for so long that many don't know the difference between a grammar rule and a style choice. Besides, grammar needn't be dry. Truly. These books are fun for those who love books and words:

- *Grammar Snobs Are Great Big Meanies: A Guide to Language for Fun and Spite* (bit.ly/GrammarSnobs) by June Casagrande. Published by Penguin.
- *It Was the Best of Sentences, It Was the Worst of Sentences: A Writer's Guide to Crafting Killer Sentences* (bit.ly/BestSentences) by June Casagrande. Published by Ten Speed Press.
- *Mortal Syntax: 101 Language Choices That Will Get You Clobbered by the Grammar Snobs—Even If You're Right* (bit.ly/MortalSyntax) by June Casagrande. Published by Penguin.
- *The Best Punctuation Book, Period* (bit.ly/PunctuationBook) by June Casagrande. Published by Ten Speed Press.
- *The Frugal, Smart, and Tuned-In Editor* blog (TheFrugalEditor.blogspot.com) is where I share wordiness tips (and others) as they occur to me.

- My *Great Little Last-Minute Editing Tips for Writers: The Ultimate Frugal Booklet for Avoiding Word Trippers and Crafting Gatekeeper-Perfect Copy* (bit.ly/Last-MinuteEditing). An inexpensive booklet for brushing up on your skills and probably a few tips that will save you some embarrassment.

For Hardcore Style Advice

There is so much disagreement about style, those who publish books need only one resource. Using too many only confuses. The recommendation below is the definitive guide for publishing *books* as opposed to online publications and newspapers and academic publications which tend to use their own style guides:

The Chicago Manual of Style (bit.ly/ChiStBk) from University of Chicago Press staff.

On Book Promotion

For basics and dozens of ideas for your book promotion campaign:

- *The Frugal Book Promoter: Second Edition* (bit.ly/FrugalBookPromo) first in my multi award-winning HowToDoItFrugally Series for writers.
- *Book Fairs for Authors* (bit.ly/DeKaysBookFairs) by Peggy DeKay. Published by Darby Press.

On Publishing

These suggestions are for authors researching available paths to publishing in this millennium and for learning self-publishing essentials.

- *Publishing Possibilities* (bit.ly/PublishingPoss) by Cheryl Pickett. A brief tutorial for authors exploring alternative paths to publishing.

For great, complete introductions to self-publishing:

- *Write, Publish, Sell!* (bit.ly/ValerieAllen) by Valerie Allen.
- *The Complete Guide to Self-Publishing: Everything You Need to Know to Write, Publish, Promote, and Sell Your Own Book* (bit.ly/MarilynRoss) by Marilyn Ross and Sue Collier.

Other Lists and Resources

- Find a long list of recommended reading on everything from editing to publishing in the appendix of the second edition of my *The Frugal Editor: From your query letters to final manuscript to the marketing of your new bestseller* (bit.ly/FrugalEditor). Also, find the list of literary agents who contributed to the chapter on literary agents' pet peeves.
- Find books for writers in all categories in the Writers' Resources pages of my Web site (howtodoitfrugally.com).
- My *SharingwithWriters* (bit.ly/SWWNewsletter) is a free e-mail newsletter that is also a community. Share your ideas. Learn from theirs! Everything from the poetry corner to promotion to craft—all frugally. Subscribe at HowToDoItFrugally.com. There is a subscription feature in the upper right corner of most every page on the site.

- My *SharingwithWriters* blog (SharingwithWriters.blogspot.com) covers book promotion, publishing, and the art of writing.
- I recently fell in love with Nina Amir's *Creative Visualization for Writers*—a kind of how and workbook. It's perfect for moving you beyond writers' block or kick-starting a new project. Subtitled *An interactive guide for bringing your book ideas and your writing career to life,* you'll find it at bit.ly/NinasVisualization.

SAMPLE QUERY and COVER LETTERS

Because query letters are important for many steps in the publishing and marketing processes, I include several examples (with permission from the authors) for you to use as inspiration.

SAMPLE QUERY LETTER:
AUTHOR TO LITERARY AGENT

I include this letter because it convinced an agent to accept *Grammar Snobs Are Great Big Meanies* and that agent sold it to Penguin. Ka-ching! Besides being an example of a letter that actually produced results, it confirms that short query letters really do sell books and reaffirms that humor can be effective.

Ms. Abkemeier:

Who among us has not, while composing a "Dear John" letter, fretted over whether to hyphenate "chronic halitosis?" What red-blooded American guy hasn't found himself at a frat party misusing the word "whom" in a vain attempt to score with a hot English major? Who can honestly say she has not, while composing a sonnet, wondered whether to put a comma between "here I sit" and "broken hearted?"

There are lots of books for dealing with this problem. Yet despite an abundance of resources, most Americans are still insecure in their use of the language. My book, *Grammar Snobs Are Great Big Meanies*, reaches out to this huge, untapped audience by serving up grammar in truly funny forms such as Al Franken-inspired spiels and David Sedaris-type yarns.

How do I know I can pull off this quintessential example of your philosophy that people buy books, "to be informed, to be entertained, or both?" Because I've been doing it successfully for more than two years as author of a humorous grammar column that appears in the *Daily Pilot* a community news supplement to the *Los Angeles Times*.

Testimonials from many readers are included in my book proposal, along with many reasons why I believe *Grammar Snobs* can outsell Lynne Truss' *Eats, Shoots & Leaves.*

I would love to send you a copy of my proposal. You can reach me via e-mail at jooon@aol.com or on my cell at XXX. I hope to hear from you soon.

Best regards,
June Casagrande

SAMPLE QUERY LETTER:
PUBLISHER OR AUTHOR TO REVIEW JOURNALS

The query letter below has a simple, professional format that independent authors can easily adapt. Notice that:

- The publisher begins with a straightforward listing of metadata.
- Pearlsong Press carefully keeps their query letters within the one-page guidelines for query letters.
- The letter does not specify what the press wants from its contact because the package adheres to *Publishers Weekly's* guidelines—meaning the book is included and it will be clear to the recipient exactly what the press (or author) is asking for.

- Rather than using all-caps for titles and other essentials, the press uses a smaller font that sets important information apart without shouting-in-type or otherwise diminishing their credibility. One of those broken rules that works.
- The letter clearly defines how this book fits into current news cycles about prejudice and defines how it adds substance to the ongoing coverage.
- The letter includes the credentials of the author.
- And last—but certainly not least—this letter from Pearlsong Press to big review journals makes it clear that the book will be given appropriate exposure in the media.

March 15, 2013

Publishers Weekly
Nonfiction Reviews
72 West 23 St. #1608
New York, NY 10010

Re: *Acceptable Prejudice? Fat, Rhetoric and Social Justice* by Lonie McMichael, Ph.D. | August 1, 2013 | 230 pp | Trade paperback $ 18.95 ISBN 9781597190657 | Ebook ISBN 9781597190640 $5.99

Fat prejudice rivals racism in American society, a study by the Rudd Center for Food Policy and Obesity has found. Yet even liberals and progressives tend to believe fat individuals don't deserve protection because fat is unhealthy and changeable—concepts supported by a great deal of societal belief and very little scientific evidence. In *Acceptable Prejudice?* Lonie McMichael uses bell hooks ideology of domination to explore the phenomena of fat prejudice and resistance to that prejudice from a rhetorical point of view. Looking at the actual experience of fat people, she argues that fat prejudice is neither acceptable nor tolerable in our society.

Lonie McMichael has a Ph.D. in technical communication and rhetoric and is teaching at the University of Colorado in Colorado Springs. She is also the author of

Talking Fat: Health vs. Persuasion in the War on Our Bodies (Pearlsong Press, August 2012).

Acceptable Prejudice? will be promoted via Internet and social media marketing, a book group guide, and author Skype availability. The original trade paperback will be available to the trade from Ingram.

You are welcome to contact me directly at peggyelam@gmail.com should you desire further information.

Sincerely,
Peggy Elam, Ph.D.
Pearlsong Press

SAMPLE COVER LETTER: FOR PACKAGE GOING TO REVIEWER

This straight forward letter was easily adapted from a query letter to a cover letter sent after a review book was requested by a review journal. It secured many reviews for David R. Yale's *Pun Enchanted Evenings* (bit.ly/PunEvening) and—by extension—many excerpts from a long list of print media including the *Little Rock Daily Record, Memphis Daily News, TCM Reviews,* and *Metroreader.*

A Healthy Relationship Press, LLC
38-11 212th Street
Bayside New York 11361-2034 USA
001-(718) 309-2656
E-mail: Media@AHealthyRelationship.com

June 22, 2010

Hilary Williamson
Book Loons
143 Lac Bois-Franc
Val-des-Monts (Québec) J8N 1C7
Canada

Dear Ms. Williamson:

We are pleased to enclose a review copy of *Pun Enchanted Evenings*: *746 Original Word Plays* (bit.ly/PunEvening). This treasury of wit, wisdom, chuckles, and belly laughs by David R. Yale will delight language lovers throughout the English-speaking world.

Midwes Book Reviews says it " . . . is a delight to read . . ." And it was given second place in the prestigious *Washington Post Style Invitational.*

Pun Enchanted Evenings, ISBN 978-0-9791766-4-7, 108 pages, 5.5" x 8.5" sells for $9.97. It is distributed by Ingram. It is also offered as an e-book in 8 different formats from smashwords.com for $5.97, ISBN 978-0-9791766-6-1.

The book is suitable for people 18+ years old. For more information, go to bestpuns.com.

The author of *Pun Enchanted Evenings,* David R. Yale, has had fiction published in *Midstream, Response,* and *Jewish Braille Review.* His *Publicity Handbook* (McGraw-Hill) was a Fortune Book Club Selection and is still in print twenty-eight years after publication. Yale studied fiction with Grace Paley at the University of Massachusetts Juniper Institute and with Joe Caldwell at the 92nd Street YMHA (Young Men's Hebrew Association).

The enclosed news release and fact sheet will tell you more about *Pun Enchanted Evenings.* Please feel free to contact me if you have any questions.

Sincerely yours,

Pat Johnson-Harte
Publisher

MEDIA RELEASE HELP

Though publicity basics like media releases are not in the purview of this book, I include one to give you an idea of how excerpts (blurbs) extracted from reviews might be used in a release to highlight the credibility of your book and capture the attention of anyone you want your release to influence.

When you send a release by post, use quality 8 ½ x 11 inch plain white paper. It should be no more than one page. Use Times New Roman font for a print release and **Verdana** for a release that will be seen online. When you e-mail a release, use "Media Release: [subject of release here]" in the subject line.

Tailor the title of your release to intrigue the media segment you feel will be most interested in your news. It might spotlight current events, use catchy language, or other techniques to make readers want to know more.

When you send your release by e-mail, use active links to your resources so your contact can click through to them easily. Because Web site addresses won't be active links when you send your release by post, underlines are superfluous. Remove them to unclutter your copy.

At the end of your release, insert three pound signs followed by a prompt for the recipient to ask for support material. It will look something like this:

###

A media kit and other support materials
are available on request at xxx@xxx.com.

Find complete information on writing media releases ("press release" is a dated term) in the second edition of my multi award-winning *The Frugal Book Promoter* (bit.ly/FrugalBookPromo). This book also explains how authors might find angles for the release of their book other than "a book has been released." Regardless of how special the release of our books feels to us authors (and even to our publishers), a new release is not generally news these days when hundreds of thousands of books are released each year. The idea of using an excerpt from a review (blurb) you see illustrated in the template on the next page might be applied to almost any release, but are most useful for poets and fiction writers.

SAMPLE GENERAL MEDIA RELEASE: FOR AN EVENT

For this media release, I chose a quote (excerpt) from a review of my novel that appeared in *The Library Journal*, arguably the most frequently used review journal used by library personnel to inform their buying public. I hoped that would influence the librarians in my city library system to recommend my book or display it prominently in each branch in the system. *Library Journal* is also a name recognized by editors and journalists from the local press as well as larger, metropolitan media, but if that weren't the case, it could easily be changed out for another blurb when I sent the release to other kinds of contacts. That choice represents only one consideration or decision you must make when you select a quote from the many reviews you will accrue.

Note: This idea of including a quotation or blurb from a review is a wee bit daring. An example of how publicists (and authors) can depart from generic templates once they know the traditions and rules, it can be used to advantage for credibility, or to give your contact a feel for your voice. Ask yourself if you have a good reason for trying something different, if what you choose helps the recipient better understand your project, or if it just feels . . . well, a little show-offy or, worse, shouts that you are ignorant of industry standards.

M E D I A R E L E A S E

Library Contact: Chuck Wikes,
Glendale Public Library Event Coordinator
Phone: XX
E-mail: XX

For Release March 06

Lecture Series Offers
Three Faces of Tolerance

"Howard-Johnson strengthens her novel with behind-the-scenes details of Mormon life and history in a book suitable for all collections, particularly those where . . . Orson Scott Card's religious books are popular. — *Library Journal*

Los Angeles, CA—Three authors known for their stand against intolerance will be guests of the Friends of the Glendale Public Library Wednesday, March 5, at 7 p.m.

at the library's central branch auditorium. The theme for the evening is "Three Faces of Tolerance."

One of the "Three Faces" is Carolyn Howard-Johnso, author of two award-winning literary books, *This Is the Place* and *Harkening: A Collection of Stories Remembered*. Both explore the corrosive nature of subtle intolerance. Another is Dr. Alicia Ghiragossian, an internationally known poet who was nominated for the Nobel Prize. Of Armenian descent, she often writes of the Armenian Genocide. Stephen Veres' memoir, *A Light in the Distance*, tells his story of survival and triumph at the beginning of WWII in Budapest, Hungary.

Library Events Coordinator Chuck Wike is pleased that "these three exceptional local authors will discuss the intercultural challenges that face our community." Howard-Johnson and Ghiragossian are residents of Glendale and Veres lives in Burbank. The event is cosponsored by the Glendale Human Relations Coalition.

Howard-Johnson's poetry and short stories appear frequently in literary journals and anthologies and she has appeared on TV and hundreds of radio stations nationwide. She also teaches classes for UCLA Extension's renowned Writers' Program.

Learn more at http://howtodoitfrugally.com .
Find her on social media:
http://facebook.com/carolynhowardjohnson
http://twitter.com/frugalbookpromo
http://pinterest.com/chowardjohnson

###

Media kits, headshots, and other support
are available upon request.

Media releases are an integral part of your media kit and media kits are part of basic publicity that is not in the purview of this book. Still, most marketing basics are essential for your pursuit of reviews. You will find directions for producing a full media kit in the second edition of my *The Frugal Book Promoter* (bit.ly/FrugalBookPromo), of course. It is important that authors learn to do it themselves or learn enough to vet a professional marketer to do it for them.

Many independent authors like children's author Darcy Pattison set up their own publishing companies complete with marketing departments (self-staffed or with a hired publicity professional) as an aid for approaching traditional media entities. Pattison says it is important for her to present her books as a publisher. Learn more about how she uses her publishing house catalog as an integral part of her media kit in Chapter Eight of this book.

APPENDIX FOUR
SAMPLE E-MAIL SIGNATURE

Automated e-mail signatures are good little helpmates. Having one saves *you* time and gives your contacts the information they need so they don't waste *their* time. Endorsements (excerpted quotations from reviews) are one of the best ways to make your signature more interesting and to give you and your title more credibility.

I break some of the supposed rules about the length of autosignatures because I am trying to set an example that being shy about accomplishments is counterproductive to the health of your book. You may find equally compelling reasons to break rules, but please—for the sake of your recipients—have the courtesy to include one with all your essential contact information.

> **Hint:** Though an e-mail address is automatically part of every e-mail one sends out, I include one in my signature as a service to those who copy and paste addresses to their contact files. It becomes a one-step process because they don't have to come back to a different part of the post to pick up the e-mail address.

> **Caveat:** Some e-mail services put up their little algorithm antennae for spam if you use too many links in your signature, so adjust your signature accordingly.

You've heard the old saying about a picture being worth a thousand words. In marketing, an image exceeds that! Here's what one of my recent e-mail signatures looks like. It's an example of how to combine a book image, an excerpt from a review, and the data that your e-mail recipient may need (or that will coax him or her into action!).

3D image by Gene Cartwright

Carolyn Howard-Johnson

"articulate, gifted, insightful, iconoclastic, and a truly impressive literary talent . . . an inherently fascinating, thoughtful, and thought-provoking read . . . *Imperfect Echoes* is highly recommended . . ." ~ Jim Cox, Editor-in-Chief of Midwest Book Review

Instructor for nearly a decade at the renowned UCLA Extension
Writers' Program.
Author of the multi award-winning series of
HowToDoItFrugally books for writers.
Amazon Profile: http://bit.ly/CarolynsAmznProfile
The Frugal Book Promoter: http://bit.ly/FrugalBookPromo
Web site: http://www.HowToDoItFrugally.com
E-mail: HoJoNews@AOL.com

Facebook: http://Facebook.com/carolynhowardjohnson
Twitter: http://Twitter.com/FrugalBookPromo
Pinterest: http://Pinterest.com/chowardjohnson

Note: If your e-mail service accommodates peek-inside widgets that combine book cover images with the ability to read an allotted number of pages, consider using the one from Bookbuzzr.com. For more on using autos signatures see Chapter Nine in this book.

OTHER FRUGAL RESOURCES FOR WRITERS

I remember how hard it was to find a publisher, participate in the galley process, and market my first book. This in spite of many years as a professional journalist, publicist, and marketer. That is why I provide so many helps for writers, many of them free. I hope they keep other writers from falling into the same potholes I did and give them the resources they need to build writing careers.

MY FREE ONLINE RESOURCES

- The Resources for Writers segment of my HowToDoItFrugally.com Web site includes several helpful lists rarely seen on other writers' portals including lists of Masters of Fine Arts programs for writers, media release disseminators, digital presses, and accessible and legitimate contests.
- *SharingwithWriters* newsletter is my free curated collection of news, opinions, and how-tos on building a writing career. It is also a community where you share your ideas and learn from others'. Everything from a poetry corner to promotion to craft to editing tips—all frugally. Subscribe at howtodoitfrugally.com. I almost always offer a little e-freebie for subscribing and subscription windows are on almost every page of my Web site in the upper right-hand corner. Find it at bit.ly/SWWNewsletter.

- My SharingwithWriters blog covers book promotion, publishing, and the art of writing and was named to Writer's Digest 101 Best Websites. (Writer's Digest's style choice is "Websites" rather than "Web sites," or "websites."). *SharingwithWriters* has its own search engine so you can find posts on the topics important to you. Find it at SharingwithWiters.blogspot.com.
- *The Frugal, Smart, and Tuned-In Editor* blog (TheFrugalEditor.blogspot.com/) is where I post information on grammar, style choices, wordiness, and pet peeves. I encourage guest posts, including yours. Read posts on things like how I flunked *Time* magazine's initialism (sometimes inaccurately called acronym) test and more.
- *The New Book Review* blog (TheNewBookReview.blogspot.com) is where authors, reviewers, and readers recycle their favorite reviews absolutely free. Follow the submission guidelines on the left of the blog homepage as carefully as you would if entering a literary contest.

THE MULTI AWARD-WINNING HOWTODOITFRUGALLY SERIES OF BOOKS FOR WRITERS

The Frugal Editor (bit.ly/FrugalEditor), Second Edition
Subtitle: *Do-it-yourself editing secrets for authors: From your query letter to final manuscript to the marketing of your new bestseller*
ISBN: 9780978515874

"Absolutely essential for beginning writers and a necessary reminder for the more advanced. The mentor you've been looking for. This book won't collect dust!" ~ Christina Francine, reviewer for *Fjords Review*

Awards: Winner USA Book News | Winner Reader Views Literary Award | Winner Next Generation Marketing Award | Finalist Next Generation Indie Book Awards | Honorable Mention Dan Poynter's Global E-Book Award

Quote from *The Frugal Editor*: "Language is a fluid lifeform. To assume that because we once learned grammar one way, it will always be accepted is fallacious. To neglect researching the language we write in when we so assiduously research the facts for what we write is folly."

There are gremlins out there determined to keep your work from being published, your book from being promoted. Resolved to embarrass you before the gatekeepers who can turn the key of success for you—they lurk in your subconscious and the depths of your computer programs. Whether you are a new or experienced author, *The Frugal Editor* will help you present whistle-clean copy (from a one-page cover letter to your entire manuscript) to those who have the power to say "yea" or "nay."

-∞-

The Frugal Book Promoter (bit.ly/FrugalEditor), Second Edition
Subtitle: *How to get nearly free publicity on your own or*

partnering with your publisher
ISBN: 9781463743291

> "Packed with wonderful information! For anyone
> who has written a book of any kind—this is a must-
> have, and must-keep guide! Every chapter is filled
> with insights and how-tos and a whole bunch of
> where-to-finds!"
> ~ Feather Schwartz Foster, author

Awards: USA Book News | The Irwin Award | Silver Award
from Military Writers Society of America | Honored by Dan
Poynter's Global Ebook Awards

For only a few cents a day *The Frugal Book Promoter* assures your book the best possible start in life. Full of nitty-gritty how-tos for getting nearly-free publicity, Carolyn Howard-Johnson, former publicist, journalist, and instructor for UCLA's Writers' Program, shares her professional experience as well as practical tips gleaned from the successes of her own book campaigns. She tells authors how to do what their publishers can't or won't and why authors can often do their own promotion better than a PR professional. The first edition is a multi award winner and the second edition is a USA Book News winner. It is updated and expanded by more than 100 pages.

–∞–

Great Little Last-Minute Editing Tips for Writers

(bit.ly/Last-MinuteEditing)
Subtitle: *The Ultimate Frugal Booklet for Avoiding Word Trippers and Crafting Gatekeeper-Perfect Copy*
ISBN-13: 9781450507653

"By creating a guide designed specifically to get writers past gatekeepers, Carolyn Howard-Johnson has created something of unmatched value: Usage advice that cuts through the contentious world of grammar to offer real help. Writers polishing their manuscripts and query letters will find Howard-Johnson's guide more useful than Strunk and White." ~ June Casagrande, author of *Grammar Snobs Are Great Big Meanies* (Penguin) and syndicated grammar columnist

This little booklet is carry-with-you protection against grammar gremlins and the frugal price of $6.95 includes a free e-book using Kindle's Matchbook program.

-∞-

The Great First Impression Book Proposal

(bit.ly/BookProposals)
Subtitle: *Everything you need to know to sell your book in 30 minutes or less*
ISBN: 9781453690956

"I just finished reading your *Great First Impression Book Proposal* . . . . I like your style and encouragement. I was a bit intimidated about finishing

315

my book proposal. I was thinking it had to be stiff and boring. I even have dialogue in mine. I thought I'd have to cut it out. Now, I'll probably leave it in." ~ Wanda Leftwich, author, blogger

The Great First Impression Book Proposal is the result of multi award-winning author Carolyn Howard-Johnson's extensive work with clients who hate writing book proposals and hate *learning* how to write them even more. She found herself coaching them through the process rather than doing it for them, for who could possibly recreate the passion an author feels for his or her own book better than the author? In doing so, she found she had written a booklet—not a tome—that took her clients only about thirty minutes to absorb. Voila! *The Great First Impression Book Proposal* was born.

This little booklet—only $6.95 out-of-pocket and thirty minutes out of a busy schedule—is part of Kindle's Matchbook program. When you buy the paperback, you get a free e-copy, too! Maybe one could be a gift for a writing friend.

SPONSORSHIPS

Advertise in Future HowToDoItFrugally Books. Contact Carolyn at HoJoNews@aol.com.

Advertise in Future HowToDoItFrugally Books. Contact
Carolyn at HoJoNews@aol.com.

SPONSORSHIP

Advertise in Future HowToDoItFrugally Books. Contact Carolyn at HoJoNews@aol.com.

SPONSORSHIP

About the Author

 Carolyn Howard-Johnson's several careers prepared her for promoting her own books and those of others. She was the youngest person ever hired as a staff writer for the *Salt Lake Tribune*—"A Great Pulitzer Prize Winning Newspaper"—where she wrote features for the society page and a column under the name of Debra Paige. That gave her insight into the needs of editors, the very people authors must work with to get free ink. Being familiar with the way news is handled helps her see how different books fit into different news cycles.

Later, in New York, she was editorial assistant at *Good Housekeeping Magazine*. She also handled accounts for fashion publicist Eleanor Lambert who instituted the first Ten-Best Dressed List. There she moved from reading effective media releases (then called press releases) to writing them for celebrity designers of the day including Pauline Trigere, Rudy Gernreich, and Christian Dior, and producing photo shoots for clients.

She has also worked as columnist, film, book and theater reviewer, and staff writer for the *Pasadena Star-News, Home Décor Buyer*, the *Glendale News-Press* (an affiliate of the *LA Times)*, Myshelf.com, and a longtime Vine reviewer for Amazon.

She learned marketing skills both in college (University of Utah and University of Southern California) and as founder and operator of a chain of retail stores. That helped her understand how authors might best partner with retailers to affect both of their bottom lines.

Howard-Johnson's experience in journalism and as a poet and author of fiction and nonfiction helped the multi award-winning author understand how different genres could be marketed more effectively. She was an instructor for UCLA Extension's renowned Writers' Program for nearly a decade and studied writing at Cambridge University, United Kingdom; Herzen University in St. Petersburg, Russia; and Charles University in Prague.

She turned her knowledge toward helping other writers with her HowToDoItFrugally series of books for writers. Her marketing campaign for the second book in that series, *The Frugal Editor*, won the Next Generation Indie Best Book Award. She also has a multi award-winning series of HowToDoItFrugally books for retailers. She says, "Marketing is marketing is marketing."

Howard-Johnson is also an award-winning novelist and poet with a the Celebration Series of chapbooks to her credit including *She Wore Emerald Then, Cherished Pulse, Imagining the Future, Blooming Red, Deeper into the Pond* and *Sublime Planet*. Jim Cox, Editor-in-Chief of *Midwest Book Review* called her most recent poetry book, *Imperfect Echoes*, "inherently fascinating, thoughtful, and thought-provoking read . . . highly recommended . . . ."

Carolyn was honored as Woman of the Year in Arts and Entertainment by California Legislature members Carol Liu, Dario Frommer, and Jack Scott. She received her community's Character and Ethics award for promoting tolerance with her writing and her city's Diamond Award in Arts and Culture. She was named to *Pasadena Weekly's* list of fourteen women of "San Gabriel Valley women who make life happen" and Delta Gamma, a national fraternity of women, honored her with their Oxford Award.

Carolyn is an actor who has appeared in ads including Apple, Lenscrafters, Time-Life CDs, Disney Cruises (Japan), and Blue Shield and is a frequent speaker at writers' conferences and tradeshows across the US.

Carolyn admits that even when she reads for pleasure she has a pencil in hand and that she edits even when she is in far-flung places like Tibet.

Author Photo by Uriah Carr

INDEX

I hope this Index makes the review process easier for you. Whenever you return to anything that is part of your promotion process involving reviews or blurbs, come here first. It will save you time scrolling through the book to find information you know is there . . . if you only knew where!

That way you can be sure you are applying the magic of reviews to whatever you are doing and in as many ways as possible. Without those cues, you may pass over the very suggestions that will help you most.

Made in the
USA
Lexington, KY